AF342601

THE FIVE SECRETS OF JAMES BOND

Alyosha Wald Lasowski

THE FIVE SECRETS OF JAMES BOND

Max Milo

Max Milo Editions, Paris, 2023
www.maxmilo.com
ISBN : 978-2-31501138-4

BIOGRAPHY

Alyosha Wald Lasowski is a university professor who teaches political philosophy at Sciences-Po Lille, in the Master's program "Philosophy, Politics, Economics".

A specialist in André Gide, Jean-Paul Sartre and Édouard Glissant, he also writes about music (*Le jeu des ritournelles*, Gallimard, 2017), painting (*Dialogue with Alain Badiou on Art and Pierre Soulages*, Cercle d'art, 2019) and cinema. His personal reflection explores an aesthetic of rhythms and a thought of tempo.

Author of fifteen books, he is also a journalist: columnist on France-Culture for the program *Avis critique*, he writes in *L'Express* for the pages "Idées".

FROM THE SAME AUTHOR

Dialogue with Alain Badiou on Art and on Pierre Soulages, Cercle d'art, 2019.

Panorama de la pensée d'aujourd'hui, volume 2, Pocket, 2019.

Le jeu des ritournelles, Gallimard, 2017.

Althusser and Us, Presses universitaires de France, 2016.

Panorama de la pensée d'aujourd'hui, volume 1, Pocket, 2016.

Édouard Glissant, thinker of the archipelagos, Pocket, 2015.

Musical Tears, William Blake & Co, 2012.

Commentary on André Gide's Faux-monnayeurs, Atlande, 2012.

Philippe Sollers, the art of the sublime, Pocket, 2012.

Jean-Paul Sartre, an introduction, Pocket, 2011.

Rythmes de l'homme, rythmes du monde (ed.), Hermann, 2010.

Jacques Rancière. Politique de l'esthétique (ed.), Archives contemporaines, 2009.

Thoughts for the new century, Fayard, 2008.

Commentary on L'enfance d'un chef *by Jean-Paul Sartre*, Gallimard, 2007.

INTRODUCTION.
A NEW LOOK AT 007

> "I think you have a secret
> that you will not tell anyone.
> Because you don't trust anyone."
> Moneypenny to 007,
> *Spectrum*

Film thinkers against James Bond

The philosophers of cinema do not appreciate the films of 007.

Stanley Cavell, American thinker of the dark rooms, specialist of the golden age of the Hollywood melodrama, deplores "this vulgar taste of the refined which characterizes James Bond" in *The projection of the world*. Gilles Deleuze for his part, who masterfully shows in *L'Image-mouvement* and *L'Image-temps* that cinema thinks in percepts and affects, or analyzes the power of color in Minnelli and the cracked crystal in Renoir, states that "the current success of James Bond seems to represent a return to a rosy conception of the secret agent" in "Philosophy of the Black Series". Roland Barthes, the author of *Mythologies*, who maintains an aesthetic game between the image-fixed - the photograph or clear room - and the image-mobile diffused by the "opaque cube" or projection room, notes that "Bond never seems to think and yet he always decides [...]. He is a beautiful object that manipulates other objects" in "Answer to a question about James Bond". As for the Slovenian neo-Marxist theorist Slavoj Žižek, a Lacanian thinker of cinema who explores the stylistic, original and traumatic leitmotif in Alfred Hitchcock's work, he evokes "the vulgar anti-communist spy thrillers of the James Bond series" in *After Emancipation*. Moreover, Slavoj Žižek points out in *Did You Say Totalitarianism?* that "the postmodern version of a James Bond film could be a kind of boring existential drama."

However, in its own way, the James Bond saga brings its touchstone to the philosophical edifice of the seventh art.

The visual work that features the secret agent 007 is neither boring nor vulgar: it announces and anticipates with virtuosity the contemporary geopolitical spectacle, upsets the conventional distinctions of masculine and feminine, or reinvents cultural codes and re-enacts social determinations. Behind the purely spectacular entertainment of the James

Bond films, behind the light, amusing and fanciful action - "pink" according to Gilles Deleuze -, the 007 saga is a popular cultural phenomenon that opens up a political space, renews an aesthetic vision and unfolds a theoretical field.

Often presented in a smooth or univocal manner, the character created by Ian Fleming in his novels is a more complex being than he appears: embodying new forms of hybridity or undecidability, 007 disrupts stereotypes, frameworks and clichés. In his own way, he questions, for example, the established relations of individual identity in a collective whole. Is he a solitary hero or an agent at the service of a group, an ideal, a community, a socio-political milieu?

A strongly constituted aesthetic figure from the outset, he renews both the spy film and the issues related to representations of the subject at the heart of globalization. With James Bond, the hierarchy between scholarly and sophisticated culture, *high culture*, and popular and standardized culture, *low culture*, disappears. As a generating and organizing principle of a cultural practice, the 007 saga modifies the frontier between the classic and the entertainment. In his sociological works Pierre Bourdieu explains that the values and the artistic tastes are internalized as determining norms by the individuals. And today, we observe more and more a displacement, a disruption, of cultural capital in a society defined more as a space of differentiation. Between legitimate or recognized art and unmentionable or forbidden pleasure, how to get out of hierarchies within a general theory of social judgment?

A hero of pure spectacle and, as such, a symbol of aesthetic equality, James Bond also participates in the renewal of democratic and popular cinema, through the reinvention of the action-image in the passage from text to screen.

Invention of the action-image

The direction and the staging of the adventures of the British secret agent mark a decisive step in the transformation of the codification of epic adventures on the big screen. In its filmic deployment, the image-action carried by the camera on 007 engages with it a visual choreography, mobilizes a graphic nervousness, builds a more and more jerky editing. Thanks to this stroboscopic process, the 007 saga re-enchants the conventional and ordinary cinema. The virtuosity is rhythmic, as - the example is among thousands - during the episode of the Junkanoo party, the local carnival of Nassau.

If the Bahamas archipelago is the enchanting setting for *Operation Thunderbolt*, James Bond finds himself surrounded in the center of the Kiss Kiss Club, the town's nightclub. While he is being chased and doing a few mambo steps, Fred Astaire in spite of himself, to the rhythm of the congas that hasten their movement, a gun appears between the curtains of the stage. The gun pointed towards the dance floor, the shooter aims and waits for the right moment. The gun, the dancers and the musical instrument, the three of them together, are swept up in the whirlwind of the fast-paced images, the frenetic music and the frenzied dancing. Then the jerky tempo stops abruptly. Musicians, dancers and images find their calm again.

A murder has taken place.

What a striking contrast to this scene, in the same film, the slow, almost slowed down, spinning of the underwater choreography! In the middle of the lagoon of Fowley Point, a new dance floor, among manta rays, octopuses and sharks, the frogmen confront each other in an aquatic ballet. The crystal clear waters are the spectacle of a strange confrontation between Heaven and Hell. The swimming beings from the infernal sea, in the service of the cruel Emilio Largo, move underwater two hydrogen bombs, the object of the ransom demanded from NATO. They are assaulted by flying beings from the air, the American parachutists of Orlando Beach, jumping from helicopters to dive into the turquoise bay of Miami. This strange silent waltz of the depths and the archipelagos, with blood colors, where scuba suits and harpoons, violence and slowness, bring its madness to the screen.

We find a stroboscopic cutting of accelerated shots during a scene from the film *Moonraker*. Accompanied by Manuela, a spy from the VH station in Rio de Janeiro, James Bond goes at night, in the middle of Carnival, to the Carlos and Wilmsberg warehouse, a subsidiary of Drax Corporation, which is located on Carioca Avenue. While the British agent explores the warehouse's crates and cargo, his local contact waits for his return and keeps an eye on the alley. Gradually, the giddiness of the urban samba takes over the bodies and the passers-by form a festive and dancing circle around Manuela. However, in the middle of the group won by the musical lightness, a worrying costumed character advances towards the spy. Suddenly, through a camera movement, the alley becomes narrow and seems to have no exit. The suspense, based on the uncertainty of the resolution and the indecision of the event, is reinforced by the alternation of images in the heart of the action between the feverish frenzy of the Brazilian dancers and the calm of the giant clown, Jaws, a cold-blooded killer with a carnivorous smile. In this scene, the spectator's feeling is divided, caught in a double atmosphere, the festive rhythm of the carnival on one side, the cold and controlled slowness of the assassin on the other. The dramatic effect is indeed a matter of editing. The suspense is born from Manuela's troubled look and the acceleration intensifies the dramatization.

All in effect of power and in search of excess, by their radical artifice and the controlled chaos of their staging, between narrative conformity and creative surprise, the films of the 007 saga develop an aesthetic of a new kind. Matter of presence and setting in movement, they compose a new plastic dramaturgy. We would like to propose here a deciphering of a new genre, also called *philoscopy*.

But what is philoscopy?

In medicine, radioscopy allows, among other things, the observation of the path of a substance in an organ, relying on new instrumentation (image intensifier, image formed on a fluorescent screen, X-ray detector, etc.) Even if it is not medical but filmic, philoscopy is inspired by new technical skills. Analyzing the image, in the service of a philosophy of the screen, makes it possible to visualize movements, to locate articulations, to underline nuances, often invisible to the naked eye. It is a reading device that deciphers camera effects in a different way.

Another reference: in psychoanalysis, the scopic drive designates both the desire to observe and the desire to be seen. This drive, discovered by Freud and associated with the sexual drive, generates a dialectic between looking and being looked at. In his work on sexuality, Freud distinguishes, in fact, the pleasure of looking and the drive to see. This distinction leads him to differentiate the eye as a biological organ of vision and the eye as a symbolic object of the drive. The word "eye" (*oculus* in Latin, *ophthalmos* in Greek, *eye* in English) becomes the incarnation of the specular image.

By investigating the memetic and visual traces of the self, Freud approaches what Henri Wallon will name "the stage of the mirror", the progressive stages of representation of the self, passage from the fragmented to the identity, from the dispersion to the identification. The specular image is constituted in a game between the seeing and the being seen. According to Freud, the three times of the scopic impulse (autoeroticism, voyeurism, exhibitionism) form the moments of the emergence of a new subject, at the same time looking and looked at, agent of a new and external look to oneself resulting from the impulse activity. This new subject is designated by Freud as "recipient of the spectacle". And the philosophical analysis of the James Bond cinema maintains the ambivalence of the scopic impulse, to make emerge a new subject, the spectator-witness. What are we looking for, by following the exploits of 007? What kind of capture is the curious and fascinated look of the spectator?

Therefore, in the anxiety-inducing climate of generalized digital surveillance, where digital observation techniques are multiplying, are the adventures of a secret agent not, in the end, a film about the gaze through the gaze itself? In the world of observation, the James Bond series leads us to question and explore the networks of control and recording. The fictional situations of the secret agent question the lie, the deciphering, the imposture, the betrayal, the ruse, the deception, the occult, the reserve, the clandestinity, the silence, the simulacrum, the dissimulation as well as the duplicity. As part of a cinematographic investigation through the eye and the gaze, through listening or hearing - from *Fenêtre sur cour* in 1954 to *Conversation secrète* in 1974, from *Blow Out* in 1981 to *La vie des autres* in 2006 -, 007's cinema also pierces the mystery of existence - true reality or false illusion? -through the opaque or obscure screen, as through a keyhole.

During his mission in Tokyo in *On ne vit que deux fois*, 007, undercover under the assumed name of Fisher, visits Osato in his company. He suspects that the director of this Japanese chemical industry is in fact a member of a criminal organization. As James Bond waits in the CEO's office, an employee in the next room is working on a robotic machine. Next to it, a small screen allows us to observe the hero's actions. Osato's accomplice and the spectator-witness will both watch 007 on this control screen connected to a security camera. This panoptic video spies on James Bond, who himself stares at and defies the camera. Strange effect of a back and forth, or of a double simultaneous observation. The camera is not one-way. It operates in two directions at the same time. It works in both directions: you look at the screen, the screen looks at you. In this scene, 007 is filmed. But is he filmed without his knowledge ?

Isn't the spy camera, whose function is to observe without being seen, a sign that no hidden bug or lens, no electronic chip or camera can detect James Bond without his noticing it? When he turns to the lens that observes him, James Bond is looking at us and scrutinizing us. Who is this "us"? Who is he looking at? His eye defies the panoptic device, the enemy agent who observes, the camera that films, the cinematographic system that constructs the narrative and the spectator who, as witness as voyeur, benefits from it. In other words, by multiplying the levels of observation, we witness, via the Freudian detour, the passage from cinemascope to cinemascopic.

By examining the action-image through the sieve of detail, the philoscopic reflection analyzes the enigma of the visual texture and offers a new dialectic of the gaze. Through a meticulous observation of the infinitesimal modulations of the narrative, the *philoscope* slips into the joints of the spy fiction.

What then can a philosophical theory of the action-image do? To avoid generalization but to focus, on the contrary, on the tiny presence of an object and the intimate movement of a gesture. The elements of the body or the decor suspend the action for a moment and expose the secret flesh of the signs. Such is the philoscopic look.

Philosophically yours

Beyond the global structure of the meaning constructed by the narrative mechanism of the film, philoscopy identifies the plays of light and shadow which, in their inventive nuances, propose another maieutic of the visible: it is not only the spectator-witness who looks at the film, but the film that looks at him, scrutinizes him and pins him down from the corner of his eye, like James Bond himself who, as a professional observer, knows that he is being observed and makes this known to the camera.

We find in *"Bons baisers de Russie"* an unusual observation instrument that illustrates the philoscopic operation wonderfully.

After a crossing by boat in the underground waters of Istanbul, 007 and Ali Kerim Bay, head of the Turkey office of MI6, go under the USSR consulate. Using a submarine periscope, ingeniously installed at the time of the evacuation of the Soviet diplomatic offices by the city's Public Works Department, in the tunnel leading from the Byzantine cistern Yetebatan Saray Sarniçi, the two men observe. Without being seen, James Bond and his friend decipher the discussions between General Vassili, director of intelligence, and Koslovski, head of security.

They cannot see the scene in its totality, but, their limited vision, scrutinize the details that the image captures. A face, a look, a gesture, the cut of a garment. They seize the unexpected of a situation, the breaks in the conversation, the brightness of an exchange. The USSR consulate becomes a movie theater, and the two heroes the film's projectionists. They make the periscope the tool of a philosophical interrogation. The shrinking of the image becomes a magnifying glass, and the accessory becomes the indispensable.

Thanks to the periscope, the reflection is as much optical and visual as theoretical and intellectual. Our tool for deciphering the 007 saga scans the anodyne element in the film and implements, at the heart of the show, the viewfinder, the very one that inaugurates every opening scene and fixes James Bond in his exchange of shots with the spectator-witness. It is the famous *gun barrel* scene: the camera is placed in the barrel of the gun, and 007 is in the center. He walks in profile, then suddenly stops, turns towards us and, in one shot, shoots his opponent.

Philosophy analyzes the power relations and political struggles that structure the saga from the following postulate: each character on the screen, in front of the camera, is a professional shooter as much as a spectator-witness who identifies his target from a defined angle. Violent, chaotic, the image-action is anticipated or accompanied by a process of fixation and determination of a target.

Every target implies a hunter and a prey. But who has this role? The fictional characters are alternately aiming and being aimed at. Several games of observation are even simultaneous, as in *Rien que pour vos yeux*. On the ski slope in Cortina d'Ampezzo, an Italian winter sports resort in the Dolomites, we watch a biathlon competition. When the GDR champion Erich Kriegler shoots his rifle during the competition, a killer with octagonal glasses, Emile Leopold Locque, can be seen behind him on the snow-covered peak. The latter observes the East German competitor through binoculars. Then, after zooming in on Locque, the camera moves directly to the center of the fourth target of the shooting event. The bullet from the rifle of Erich Kriegler, a sports competitor and hitman, hits and explodes the target. But who did he shoot? Once again, the spectator-witness is the target. And not James Bond, who watches the scene with Olympic skater Bibi Dahl, watches the sporting feat and then applauds the shooting as if it were a carnival game. But this game is short-lived. The hero does not stay in suspense for long: James Bond is Kriegler's next target.

Why are representations shaken up, in a spy film that uses the target as a frame for the action-image? The *filmoscopic* ethic establishes a synchronization between the angle of view of the image and the perception of reality, a correspondence between the visual frame and the physical engagement in the world. The aesthetic delimitation of the shot becomes, for the time of a film, a space of truth and the deployment of the secret. By its movement the image-action establishes the fictitious place of the real.

In *Goldfinger,* the gangster meeting at Auric Goldfinger's Kentucky ranch takes place in front of a reconstructed model of Fort Knox. All the details of the ultra-militarized buildings of the largest gold reserve in the United States, with fifteen billion dollars in its vaults, are reproduced in miniature. During Goldfinger's briefing, and the lecture-like exposition of his criminal project, with maps and images to support it, the viewer can make out James Bond's eyes, which appear through the rods of the model. Under the floor, trapped between tiny bars, 007 is reduced to his eyeballs.

Here he is, like another Gulliver, now a shrunken or diminished man. This human condition of miniaturization allows him to clandestinely observe the scene during which Goldfinger exposes the "Grand Slam" operation prepared during fifteen years of his life by the crook.

The panoptic power of the camera

In the films of the 007 saga, the discovery of the world - the observation of reality - is based on a concentration of the beams of perception which conditions the unfolding of the images. In optics, this is called a "spectrum". Beyond its scientific name, this physical term, the visual prism of a luminous radiation, refers to two other meanings. On the one hand, it evokes an ectoplasmic and ghostly floating phenomenon, a furtive ghost that haunts and a spirit without a body that returns, the object of a spectrographic analysis; on the other hand, this term designates a particularly dangerous, particularly effective criminal organization, named "Spectre", with which James Bond is regularly confronted.

The use of artifice is the condition of the glance. No revealing vision without artifact. Is this not the panoptic power of the camera, as Michel Foucault shows it in relation to the disciplinary society? And "this surveillance is based on a permanent recording system," writes the philosopher in *Surveiller et punir*, in 1975. How many screens are thus mobilized in the 007 saga to realize this process!

When, in *On ne vit que deux fois*, James Bond finds himself on the metal slide that lands him directly on the chair of Tanaka's office, the head of the Japanese secret service is amused by such an easy capture. The two men, who immediately sympathize, watch together, in retrospect, the unfolding of the previous sequence, as far as video screens have recorded the hero's movements in the subway corridors. How better to display, by interposed screens, this idea that the image is constantly controlled, viewed, recorded?

But, beyond the paradigms of control and surveillance, the eye can also spot, in the concentration of a seizure, an insignificant or minor element. Every pure diamond detail then appears in this tightening: Bond's scar on his lower back, Solitaire's velvety shoulder, Honey Rider's two bare feet on the sand, the ring on the finger of a player drawing a card during a game of baccarat. It is the fold of the image that makes the quality of the film, as Robert Bresson points out in his *Notes on the Cinematograph*: "A sigh, a silence, a word, a sentence, a commotion, a hand."

The philoscopy accompanies the discretion of a minimal event, and makes manifest what is not completely hidden, but expelled by the heart of the image to the margins of the vision. By an operation of dejoining and disjunction, the reading of the film allows what constitutes "the under-seen" of the image to emerge, as we speak elsewhere of "the implied", of what, too quickly, too often, is passed under silence.

Isn't this the hero's most important quality? Being a keen observer allows James Bond to deceive appearances. Did you notice, in the opening of *Operation Thunderbolt,* that under the widow's black clothes is Colonel Jacques Bouvard? Observed by Bond from the balcony during the funeral ceremony in the church, the murderer of two of his MI6 colleagues is mourning his own funeral, disguised as a darkly dressed woman. The deception does not escape the secret agent.

No secret seems to remain hidden to this trained eye. His sense of capture allows Bond to be simultaneously actor and observer, spectator and director, watcher and watched. Nothing escapes him: James Bond is definitely the thinker of philosophy.

Museum theft: Julius No did it

Captured with Honey Rider on the mysterious Caribbean island of Crab Key, off the coast of Jamaica, 007 observes the ocean floor through a 25 mm convex glass magnifying glass. The thick glass of the aquarium puts the spy-agent face to face with the fish that look at him with curiosity. This mise en abyme is a mise en abysse. Just as there are clown fish, is James Bond not himself a spy fish swimming in the film's vast aquarium?

Architect of his own fortress, for which he designed the plans, Doctor No shows his prisoners the refinement of his living room, an underwater sanctuary. But James Bond provokes him: "Sardines disguised as whales, like you on your island." To which No replies, "It all depends on which side of the magnifying glass you're on." A final, very appropriate reflection, which marks the exchanges of the observed-observer.

A few moments later, invited to follow their jailer, 007 and Honey Rider climb the steps to go to the table of the dining room, in order to have dinner with their bloody host. Stopped in his dash, the hero stops a moment in front of the steps. He observes a painting, which, exposed on the screen, strangely stares at the spectator.

What is this painting, which piques the curiosity of the secret agent and ours, at the crucial moment when Doctor No is going to reveal his plan to his prisoners? It is a copy of the Duke of Wellington's portrait, a painting by Goya in 1813.

Belonging to the National Gallery in London, the painting was stolen in 1961, during the shooting of the film. The theft of the portrait made the headlines in London.

In a nod to current events, the Goya painting was finally found in 1965, in the locker room of Birmingham station, after an anonymous letter was sent to the police with a locker slip announcing the place and location of the stolen painting. As soon as they arrived on the spot according to these indications, the Scotland Yard investigators discovered the painting, wrapped in a package covered with a wrapping cloth.

Could Dr. No have been the one who ordered the robbery, and did the 1962 film *James Bond vs. Dr. No* already taunt the police by giving them a precious clue on camera? In any case, this detail, specular for the philosophic eye and spectacular for the media eye, invites itself on the Jamaican island, and diverts for a moment the gaze of the hero and the spectator towards another police news.

This is the invitation - the challenge - that we are given to pierce the mystery, so it is up to us to reveal now, through our philosophical investigation, the five secrets of James Bond. Who is really 007?

Philoscopy of the spy agent

Through the angle of a viewfinder, as precise and detailed as possible, the philoscopic gaze allows us to break with the obvious and to go beyond appearances, by targeting and revealing five secrets about James Bond.

The first mystery concerns the links between the spy's exploits and geopolitics. How does the 007 saga anticipate the contexts and situations of the Cold War and the post-Cold War era? How does the character evolve, in the face of the impending international situation, the backdrop of espionage, from the conflict between the East and West blocks, to the tension in Europe caused by Britain's *Brexit*? Closely intertwined with the confrontation between the USSR and the United States, the adventures of James Bond are not a mere product of the confrontation between the great powers, but play a real role in it. In their own way, not only do the films foreshadow on-screen events that will occur in reality, but they also decentralize and depolarize geopolitical issues. How does fiction embody and displace the global political order? On the one hand, James Bond promotes rapprochement, understanding and cooperation between the forces of the Atlantic Alliance and those of the Warsaw Pact; on the other hand, very early in the saga, 007 is certain that the enemies are elsewhere. The stakes of the post-September 11 world are not far. Ahead of the upheavals taking place on the planet, the secret agent faces enemies with new faces: cyberwarfare, *fake news*, criminal bankers, eco-terrorists in the service of multi-nationals or pharmaceutical companies.

The second secret concerns James Bond's cosmopolitan yet British identity. If he acknowledges his faithful attachment to the British crown and his fervor in serving the Queen, isn't the spy 007 also a citizen of the world, beyond all borders and territories? Mixing a multiple hybridity with the classical symbols of the British subject, the films of the saga question the notions of border, belonging and post-national identity in rupture with a strict territorial vision, linked to his sincere commitment to MI6. The hero's citizen subjectivity is open to different linguistic microclimates, sensitive to multiple cultures and manifests a plasticity in the circulation of representations. Is this a form of postmodernity, embodied then by the deterritorialized individual, as opposed to a more classical vision of the subject?

The third secret questions the film of love in the spy film, through the relations of seduction between men and women in the 007 saga. By turns hedonist, dandy, romantic or passionate, is James Bond reduced to the sole incarnation of ordinary male virility? Is he only a being of pleasure, enjoyment and easy success with women? If we look at James Bond films differently, more through the aesthetics of romantic melodrama or Hollywood love comedy, we can observe the free play of marivaudage, libertinage, banter and gallant seduction. Despite his very assertive masculinity and misogyny, James Bond experiences love, goes through existential crises and questions his feminine ideal. In his multiple attempts at seduction, can we not read in them a permanent hope of the marriage to come? An original conception of the couple and an authentic vision of feminism emerge, in connection with the #MeToo and Time's Up movements. Turning on himself, Agent 007 disrupts the male paradigm and even embodies a critical distance from the conventional man. How does the hero, in the service of a noble cause and the common good, manage his physical and emotional vulnerability? Moreover, clues invite us to consider his possible bisexuality.

The fourth enigma refers to the place of the hero's body in the cinematographic image. What are the stages of Bond's bodily metamorphosis, whose main function as a secret agent is physical exploit or muscular action? From real appearance to imaginary plasticity, 007 engages a presence of two orders, both concrete and immediate, but also dreamed and fantasized. Bond belongs simultaneously to two worlds, on the one hand the world of espionage, on the other hand the world of the image. This double belonging casts doubt on the unity of his physical and corporeal being. Haunted by death and resurrection, 007 is a ghostly being. He has become a surreal, spectral and ectoplasmic figure. The hero pushes the metaphysical limits of the separation between life and death. What survivor is he?

The fifth and final secret leads to the detection of all the cultural references that form the basis of the hero's style and determine the universe of his adventures. On the one hand, Bond's singular tastes, through his musical, gastronomic or clothing preferences. On the other hand, the set of cultural markings that run through the films, and that associate classical culture with contemporary values, from Chopin to the

Beatles or the Beach Boys. If we look closely, we can see in the films an art of quotation and collage, from François de La Rochefoucauld to Charles Spencer Chaplin, Steven Spielberg and Stanley Kubrick, or through the winks or allusions to the films *Lawrence of Arabia* by David Lean or *Casablanca* by Michael Curtiz. So, are the films of the Bond saga revealing a classic espionage universe, or do they compose more of a pop world in pulp style?

The philoscopic reading attempts to reveal five secrets at the heart of the adventures of one of the most famous heroes of film culture. To achieve this, only the detail of a camera-target, as precise as possible, can reveal the unexpected under the predictable, the incredible under the believable, the surprising under the plausible.

With the help of the philoscopic viewer, which allows us to look at the twenty-five films of the James Bond saga, from 1962 to 2020, with fresh eyes, it is the whole series that we must take into account. And this "series" is to be understood as the twenty-six cathedrals of the painter Monet: not only an accumulation of singular films, but effects of echoes, of cross-references, a secret logic of generation that draws under the flashy fresco an unsuspected landscape.

1. Beyond East and West: *Game save the Queen*

"Holly Goodhead:
I hate being spied on, Mr. Bond!
James Bond:
Nobody likes that, right?"
Moonraker

How is contemporary geopolitics anticipated and foreshadowed by the films of the 007 saga? From the post-war 1950s to the *Brexit* crisis, from the Cold War to the European question, from the fall of colonial empires to terrorist violence, each James Bond film constitutes an aesthetic paradigm for thinking about the world immediate to it and for accompanying the upheavals of its time. But if the James Bond series illustrates contemporary events, can it also influence and transform them? Of which heralding policy is "James Bond" the name?

Great Britain, year zero

A glamorous pop icon, the James Bond character was created by Ian Fleming in 1953.

A year earlier, on a sunny morning in his Jamaican home by the sea, Ian Fleming sat at his desk in front of his portable Imperial typewriter. A hot coffee in one hand and his cigarette holder ready to be lit in the other. Sitting in a wooden armchair, with some equestrian engravings on the wall in front of him. His house, built according to his own plans and named "Goldeneye", is surrounded by a flowery estate where mimosa grows in abundance. Educated at the best schools in England, Ian Fleming was successively a journalist, stockbroker and chief of staff at the British Admiralty, where he served as undercover coordinator and liaison officer. Now he uses his spare time to write, as his brother Peter already does.

Naturally imaginative and observant, Ian Fleming liked to browse his personal library. That day, like so many other mornings, he leafed through a few books to find new sources of inspiration. He opened the first book, a short story by Rudyard Kipling, written in 1897, in which the characters are steam locomotives. The title of this short story, named after the number of one of the railway engines, intrigues him: *007*.

Further down the shelves, Fleming took pleasure in discovering the illustrated plates of *Birds of the West Indies*, an ornithological volume devoted to several hundred species of birds living in the Caribbean Sea. He liked the name of the zoologist who wrote this animal book. It was called "James Bond". That was all it took to trigger his creative spirit: Ian Fleming plunged into writing an epic and popular work.

In twelve novels and nine short stories, Ian Fleming revolutionized spy literature. The first adventure of his hero, *Casino Royale*, which quickly became a literary phenomenon, appeared in bookstores shortly after, in 1953.

1953 was also the year of the coronation of the young Queen Elizabeth II at the age of twenty-five. This event, made planetary by television, inaugurated a new era of the British monarchy as well as a new media era. Thanks to sophisticated technical means and a technological feat, the ceremony had a global reach: an unprecedented process, set up by the BBC, allowed nearly seventy cameras to broadcast the coronation live to television stations around the world.

The first production in mondovision had an exceptional impact and allowed twenty-seven million English people and two hundred and eighty million television viewers to attend the celebration, as a manifestation of the royal splendor and glory.

In the same year, an unbreakable bond was forged between James Bond and the Queen, who both embodied the radiant renewal of Great Britain. This rebirth comes as a sudden light, after the years of sacrifice and mourning during the dark hours of the Second World War.

From a more intimate point of view, a deep relationship of closeness unites James and Elisabeth who share the same longevity, from that time and throughout the films that will follow, until ours.

Thus, when he goes through a difficult episode of his profession as a spy, at the time of his quick and brutal resignation from MI6, while he has just dictated the letter to Miss Moneypenny, in *Her Majesty's Secret Service*, in 1969, James Bond has only one thought and this thought is for the Queen.

Throughout the scene, James Bond is alone, silent, plagued by doubt and melancholy. Busy tidying his drawers and emptying his desk, he is immersed in the memory of his past missions, and brings out the symbolic accessories of his previous actions. He finds again the knife of Quarrel, the watch-cable of strangulation or the waterproof mini respirator. Suddenly thinking that these might be his last acts in arms, Bond takes out a bottle of alcohol, puts it to his lips and turns to the painting of Elizabeth II, then a young queen in full regalia. On the screen, the image of the sovereign is superimposed on that of James Bond, creating a complicity and the exchange of a dialogue. Raising his bottle as a sign of homage, he addresses the queen and presents her with these words of farewell: "Pardon Madame, a thousand regrets."

This scene from 1969 with its melodramatic tone renews 007's attachment to the Queen.

But let's go back a bit. Nine years after his literary creation, the secret agent in the service of Her Majesty was born a second time, in this case on film. In 1962, James Bond made his appearance on the silver screen. The world premiere of *James Bond vs. Doctor No takes place* in London on October 5. The film adventure begins.

After the first birth, in 1953, which sealed 007's loyalty to the Queen, the second birth, in 1962, was accompanied by a global strategic upheaval. A geopolitical coup de théâtre plunges James Bond's fiction into the heart of international reality.

At that time, at the time of the film's release, a large-scale secret military operation was taking place, launched four days earlier in the greatest secrecy. Under the code name of Operation Kama, the Kremlin ordered seven Soviet submarines, armed with torpedoes and nuclear missile launchers, to be sent to Cuba. The American ship *Yerkon,* attached to the military activities of maritime transport, which detected this abnormal activity, spotted the movement of one of the attack submarines and transmitted its signal to the base and command forces of the US Navy.

Washington goes on alert.

A few days later, while the first visual adventures of 007 were a popular success at the cinema, aerial photographs were taken by an American U2 spy plane. The images confirm the Pentagon's fear: the Soviets are setting up a launch base for nuclear-tipped rockets on the island of Cuba, within easy reach of Florida, in the direction of Miami and major American cities. These revelations set the world on fire.

James Bond vs. Doctor No tells the story of how, for fear of missile *toppling* - destruction by telescoping or hijacking by radar jamming - the American secret service entrusts their British counterparts with the mission of protecting the rockets' takeoff from Cape Canaveral. As if to prevent the same thing from happening in reality, President John Fitzgerald Kennedy also organized a crisis cell at the White House.

The character of James Bond is born in the cinema while the world trembles and holds its breath. As 007 investigates Doctor No's disturbing experiments with radioactivity and discovers his plan for destructive madness, the risk of nuclear war on a global scale is imminent in 1962 between the two superpowers. For the General Secretary of the Communist Party of the Soviet Union, Nikita Khrushchev, the Americans were responsible for the aggravation of the tension of the Cold War. The maneuvers of the USSR in the Caribbean Sea were only a response to the threat deployed against it in Europe, where the United States installed fifteen *Jupiter* rockets in Turkey and thirty in Italy, all aimed at Russia and its allies.

On the White House side, discussions are lively within the National Security Council. Robert McNamara, the Secretary of Defense, and Curtis LeMay, the Chief of Staff of the US Air Force, were both in favor of military intervention in response to the Russian provocation and tried to convince Kennedy to strike hard. But the President of the United States was not in favor of retaliation and preferred negotiation and dialogue with the Politburo. It was necessary to find a common ground and avoid the escalation of nuclear threats.

On the side of reality as on the side of fiction, it is the same urgency: time is running out. The clock is ticking. Missions can only be successful if they stay on schedule and operate efficiently in a short time. Every secret agent knows this. It is a question of tempo. Time is against you.

In 1962, under the cover of Universal Exports, a London-based import-export trading company, James Bond soon meets Pleydelle-Smith, the first secretary to the governor of Jamaica. His investigation into the disappearance of MI6's local Kingston contact, Commander John Strangways, leads Bond to explore the small offshore islands of Fine Island, Morgan's Reef and Crab Key. Pressed by the urgency of the matter, 007 receives a Geiger counter, arrived from London by diplomatic bag, in order to inspect the stone samples from bauxite and pyrite mines collected by Strangways. The local press, through the intermediary of a journalist who works freelance for the *Daily Gleaner,* tries to find out more from the secret agent. The pressure mounts on the side of MI6 and the Ministry of Defense to discover the origin of the radioactivity. The same imperative for results in 1962 for the international political reaction of the West: after the submarines, Soviet ships were on their way to Cuba to deliver the material for the installation of missile bases.

Tensions rise when an American surveillance plane is shot down over the Caribbean Sea. The third world war is ready to break out. Havana was also on the warpath, after the failure of the attempted landing organized by the CIA in 1961 in the Bay of Pigs against its leaders. With American support, Cuban opponents of Lider Máximo Fidel Castro tried, in vain, to land on the island to overthrow the political regime. Cuba then chose its side, anti-imperialist and against the U.S. leadership. To resolve the conflict of the missile crisis, Kennedy had to make a decision: he imposed an embargo on Cuba, hoping, through this blockade, to prevent Russian ships from landing on the island.

While the world is watching this perilous game between Washington, Havana and Moscow, what is London doing? What has happened to British diplomacy and its geopolitical influence at the heart of international relations? Since Winston Churchill's resignation in 1955, there has been radio silence. The London answer comes from the immediate success of James Bond's adventures. Quickly becoming a popular hero, 007 embodies the surge of reaction that counterbalances the progressive decline of British power.

In December 1962, a few weeks after the film's release, the Bahamas conference demonstrated the American desire for hegemony and monopolistic control of Western nuclear power. During the negotiations, the Kennedy administration obtained from the British Prime Minister, Harold Macmillan, the abandonment of the *Skybolt* ballistic missile project and its replacement by *Polaris* rockets, supplied and manufactured by the Americans. The conclusion of the Nassau agreements was clear: vulnerable and weakened, the British military force lost its nuclear autonomy and was placed under the authority of the NATO High Command.

Faced with this risk of Atlanticization, Great Britain is trying to face up to it on the European scene. It intended to restore the image of its power, in particular by modernizing its aeronautical fleet, even if this concerned only the civilian, and not the military, domain. On November 29, 1962, the French and British governments signed an agreement in London for the joint development of a supersonic civil transport aircraft, named "Concorde". The Franco-British treaty was a historic event, the most important in European aeronautics, both in terms of the technical progress made and the strengthened cooperation between neighboring countries.

But this is still far from being politically sufficient. For, after the humiliating affront of the Nassau Agreement, Britain suffered a new blow to its policy of foreign sovereignty. The special ties within the Commonwealth - which in the early 1960s consisted of twenty-nine independent states, six associated countries and thirty annexed territories - were disrupted. Great Britain's position in the world was shifting. National interests and political implications are once again at stake. What was going on? In 1962, fiction and reality are once again mirrored.

On the one hand, *James Bond vs. Doctor No* has as its opening scene a problem of interrupted telephone and radio connection between the frequency W6N Jamaica (transmitted from the "Letter Box" in Commander Strangways' private residence in Kingston) and that of G7W London (the communication wave from the radio control of the MI6 offices in England). On the other hand, relations within Her Majesty's empire were also breaking down: Jamaica, a British colony since 1670, gained its independence in August 1962, as did the Cayman Islands, Turks and Caicos, the states of Uganda and Trinidad and Tobago.

London did try to maintain a semblance of unity among the Commonwealth countries with the creation of the British West Indies Federation in 1958. But in 1962, the British West Indies Federation, which had included Jamaica, Trinidad and Tobago, Dominica, St. Lucia, Antigua and Barbuda, Barbados, St. Christopher and Nevis, St. Vincent, Grenada and the Grenadines, and Montserrat, was dissolved.

Jamaica seceded, which is precisely the island where Ian Fleming took up residence to write his novels, the place where he installed his luxurious villa. This vast house, with its tropical garden facing the ocean, called "Goldeneye", received in 1956, in the middle of the Suez crisis, Prime Minister Anthony Eden and his wife, Countess Clarissa Churchill, niece of Winston Churchill. But in 1962, the Caribbean no longer responded. A communication problem, no doubt.

Secession hits Great Britain.

James Bond's commitment to the service of England during the Cold War is the best answer to the doubt and fragility that are winning the hearts of the British people. He is the only one who has the strength to react, in the face of the famous and severe judgment of the diplomat and former American Secretary of State Dean Acheson: "Britain has lost an empire and has not yet found a role." This cruel sentence was uttered on December 5, 1962, just as on the screens Bond gave a new impetus to England.

Murder in an English Garden

In the early 1960s, James Bond raised the profile of politics in Britain. His arrival on the silver screen gave the intrepid and troubled Albion unexpected support. What about some sixty years later, today, in 2020, for 007's twenty-fifth appearance? Does his role in the film saga still resonate with current events?

If the world has changed today, international tension seems to have resumed in earnest. The nuclear threat has not stopped: in October 2019, North Korea renewed this threat and announced missile tests. A few days later, also in October 2019, the United States sells Ukraine *Javelin* anti-tank missile launchers, in order to maintain pressure on Russia, after a conversation between President Trump and his Ukrainian counterpart Zelensky.

Where is James Bond? After twenty-four films of good and loyal service, the spy can legitimately deserve a retirement, or at least a break in his activities to defend the planet. He hopes that England will give him a break and not count on him to save the free world alone.

This is what the opening of *Dying Can Wait* announces. The original title of the twenty-fifth film, *No Time to Die*, should logically translate into "No time to die" - while "Pas un temps pour mourir" would be the adaptation of *Not a time to die*. At the beginning of the twenty-fifth episode of the saga, James Bond is enjoying peaceful days in Jamaica, where he has retired, tired and worn out by so much action, before a new mission, from his friend and CIA agent Felix Leiter, whom he met fifty-eight years earlier on the Kingston harbor docks in *James Bond vs.*

James Bond tired? Let's remember that, since the 2000s, 007 faces new adversaries, each one tougher than the last. His enemies are multiple: press tycoon, terrorists linked to the oil or water empire, North Korean military, banker of international terrorism, secret organizations, and also computer hackers who propagate *fake news* and disinformation.

If James Bond is looking for a little rest, it is also because England is once again in turmoil. Britain is going through a new storm, this time far removed from the Cold War, but with risks just as great. On June 23, 2016, the United Kingdom voted in a referendum in favor of *Brexit* at 51.8%, with 17.4 million votes cast in favor of a net detachment from the European Union.

This political result is a global thunderclap, a real concussion on a European scale. The *Brexit* triggers a deep international political crisis, which could break up the bloc of twenty-seven EU member countries. In England, Prime Minister David Cameron, who organized the vote and was in favour of remaining in the EU, immediately resigned.

The outcome of the referendum paralyzed the country: the national economy was blocked, the entire British political class was torn apart, and the press was at loggerheads. Since Britain joined the European Union on January 1, 1973, nothing has ever been simple, as shown by its refusal to adopt the single currency in 1999. But now the country seems to be losing its bearings and its stability. The substitution of referendum democracy for parliamentary democracy is having unexpected consequences.

In March 2017, the Westminster Parliament definitively passes the bill that authorizes the legal activation of the *Brexit*. The same year, the new "Iron Lady" and British Prime Minister, Theresa May, relies on Article 50 of the Lisbon Treaty, which regulates the departure of a member of the Union. The tenant of *10 Downing Street is* organizing the exit procedure, in order to separate the United Kingdom from the other twenty-seven states. What does *Brexit*, for "Britain exit", mean to its supporters? Is it a sign of a return to pure British sovereignty, to a rediscovered national island identity, or is it a desire to deregulate the economy in the face of directives from Brussels and to promote greater liberal and commercial fluidity? In the general political context that accompanies the release of *Mourir peut attendre*, a new page is turned for England. Another symbol: Prince Philip, husband of Queen Elizabeth II, officially retires in August 2017, at age 96, during his last review of the Royal Marines parade in Buckingham.

Faced with the popular unrest that is shaking England, Queen Elizabeth II gives her official approval to wait and postpone the *Brexit* as far as necessary.

The signs of destabilization are obvious: exceptional closure of parliamentary sessions, regular suspension of the British Parliament, frequent resignations of public figures, such as John Bercow, Speaker of the House of Commons, petitions and pressure from MPs in the face of the threat of dissolution of the Assembly. Can we talk about political chaos? The impact of an "exit without agreement" is seen as a major political danger.

At the origin of this chaos, Prime Minister Boris Johnson. If the *Brexit* were the script of a movie-catastrophe, the ex-journalist, former mayor of London and foreign minister from 2016 to 2018 would be the main evil character. Half-clone half-clown of Donald Trump, he imitates in every way his American populist model. Against the political elites of his country, he proclaims himself the sole representative of the British people. With the prospect of a *no deal*, Boris Johnson brandishes the threat of an exit without an agreement. He is also violently attacking the institutions, wishing to weaken the European authorities, from the Supreme Court to the courts in Brussels, which want to stop his frenzy.

His strategy of provocation and confrontation makes Boris Johnson the perfect incarnation of the evil figure. He would be the designated adversary of 007: Boris Johnson has the greed and pride of Auric Goldfinger, the unbridled ambition of domination of Max Zorin, develops the sense of manipulation and destabilization of Silva. His obsession with power plunges the country into doubt: a broken kingdom, a weakened democracy, a divided society. With, in particular, the fear of a new border between Northern Ireland, attached to the United Kingdom, and the Republic of Ireland, member of the European Union.

As the London newspaper *The Guardian* explains, "This country that prided itself on being stable, tolerant and moderate, with a crown that symbolizes traditions honed over centuries, is proving fragile and fiercely divided." Boris Johnson's disregard for legal and constitutional rules is leading him to destroy the transitional balance and turn the United Kingdom into a European Singapore. Encouraging every man for himself, practicing social and fiscal dumping, manipulating public opinion: Boris Johnson's political methods echo the projects of destruction and annihilation set up by the evil figures of excessive ambition that James Bond confronts in his adventures, such as the ruthless Karl Stromberg or the terrifying Hugo Drax.

In his dialogue with Truffaut, Hitchcock recalls this fundamental principle of cinema: "The more successful the villain, the more successful the film. That is the great cardinal rule. If we follow this advice, Boris Johnson would be a very successful villain. Since he came to power, there has been unprecedented instability and fragility in the UK. The British economy is a victim of many crises: for the first time in its history, the airline British Airways suffers a general strike in September 2019, followed by the cancellation of its eight hundred and fifty daily flights, costing the company forty-four million euros per day. The same catastrophic situation with the bankruptcy in September 2019 of the oldest tour operator in the world, the British agency Thomas Cook, whose London-based parent company is in receivership.

Faced with the chaos of *Brexit*, James Bond has a strong opponent in the person of Boris Johnson. Moreover, as is often the case between the most bitter opponents, the two men have something in common: James Bond, in fiction, and Boris Johnson, in reality, were both educated at the same school, Eton College, near London, a mecca of English elitist education, founded by King Henry VI. But the one of the two who was quickly expelled from this institution is not necessarily the one you think of.

The challenge between the two men remains. In London, at a Conservative Party conference, political leader Boris Johnson vowed, "Make *Brexit* happen or die." Faced with this challenge, the agent James Bond responded directly to him, as a warning, with the title of his twenty-fifth film: *Dying Can Wait*. Seventy-four years after Winston Churchill's speech in Zurich in 1946 on the project of the "United States of Europe", the divorce is pronounced between the United Kingdom and the European Union. On January 31, 2020, the Union Jack will disappear from the twenty-eight European flags. Forty-seven years after joining the EEC on January 1, 1973, and almost four years after the referendum of June 23, 2016, the United Kingdom and its sixty-six million inhabitants can sing the Beatles' 1967 pop tune, "I say no and You say stop. The song concludes with "I don't know why you say good bye".

La dolce morte

Throughout the Cold War and the post-Cold War era, up to our time with his most recent adversaries, James Bond embodies the defense of the free world. 007 protects the values of democracy and justice, facing threats of annihilation and destructive madness. Against violence, terrorism, dictatorship and totalitarianism, he defends all individual freedoms: Western culture, political freedom, liberal democracy and human rights. For decades, James Bond has represented the values of the Western system in the face of the danger of Sovietism in the East.

James Bond fights for the protection of freedom and confronts the most terrible threats to modern, humanistic and tolerant society. An ideal figure of Britishness and Anglicity, he is the quintessential Anglo-Saxon secret agent and Western spy in the service of peace, culture and brotherhood.

As an ally of the United States and protector of Europe, James Bond's career reflects this political commitment. As a young man, he joined the Britannia Royal Naval College, then the Special Boat Service. He then worked for the Defence Intelligence Staff, before being recruited to MI6, the British foreign secret service, attached to the Ministry of Intelligence and founded in 1909. A member of the private London club "The Circle of Ambassadors", Bond was also a *Commander* in the Navy and a Knight of the Military Order of St. Michael and St. George.

A member of the espionage elite, he holds the rank of "00" agent, which gives him a great deal of autonomy in his various functions as well as a strong responsibility for success: investigation, intelligence, diplomacy, solving disappearances, searching for information, making contact with the enemy, confronting the opposing side, protecting civilian populations, freeing the innocent, taking large-scale action in the face of hostage-taking or intervening effectively against threatening and dangerous enemies. The international missions of the secret agent are always aimed at protecting the individual and society. Integral and respectful of these great political principles, James Bond is faithful to tradition and concerned to follow the general framework of his mission instructions. He adapts to the circumstances, often preferring to rely more on his sensitivity and instinct than on the strictest orders. Ready to sacrifice himself, the spy puts himself in danger for the common good. He embodies chivalrous heroism. When his boss asks him to give up his usual weapon, Bond obeys. He agrees to give up his Beretta, and to replace it with the Walther PPK 7.65 mm, with a Brausch silencer, even though, as 007 knows, his Beretta has been effective for ten years. Bond adapts. On the other hand, in another situation, after attending a music concert at the Bratislava Opera House, when Saunders, head of Section V in Vienna, orders Bond to shoot the armed cellist Kara Milovy, 007 disobeys and disarms her, only by aiming at the butt of his gun.

To carry out the missions entrusted to the British secret service, the geopolitical rapprochement and complicity make MI6 and the CIA, the central intelligence agency of the United States, natural allies. James Bond is frequently assisted by his friend and accomplice, Felix Leiter, who regularly accompanies him, present from the first adventure, *James Bond against Doctor No*, as in the twenty-fifth, *Dying Can Wait*. This friendly and professional relationship shows the CIA agent as a sympathetic character, but less insightful and effective than the spy of MI6: during a joint mission near the port of Kingston, in *James Bond against Doctor No*, the difference is obvious. With a jacket over his shoulder and an obvious air of casualness, Felix Leiter walks up to his friend James Bond on the harbor quay and asks him "Did you lose something?", while at the same time 007 is taking radioactive readings at the seaside on a boat with the proper equipment and materials. In another mission, investigating together in *Goldfinger*, Leiter's attitude illustrates American consumer society. While

James Bond pursues the mission inside Goldfinger's Kentucky ranch, Felix Leiter observes him from the outside, thanks to a *homer*: 007 hides a radio transmitter in the heel of his shoe, allowing the CIA to track his movements by picking up the direction of the signal through a receiver in Leiter's car. But Leiter, while observing the signals on his dashboard, also spends his time enjoying a chicken sandwich at *Colonel Sanders' recipe* or *Joe's drive-in Restaurant*. And when the agent and his second-in-command approach the ranch with binoculars to find out where Bond is, the two CIA men are quickly spotted by Goldfinger, who mistakes them for meddling and clumsy turfers.

In general, beyond the case of Felix Leiter, American agents do not always have the speed and accuracy of their British counterparts. In *On ne vit que deux fois*, when an unidentified spacecraft seizes the American shuttle *Jupiter-16* in space, an international diplomatic summit meeting is held to deal with the crisis. Worried about this threat, the United States accuse the Soviet government which guarantees in answer its will of peace. Faced with the growing tension between the two countries around the negotiating table, Britain interferes: "For what purpose would our Russian friends attack a U.S. spacecraft?" The British diplomat continues his analysis: if Great Britain does not believe that the pirate shuttle is Russian, thanks to its counter-intelligence services, it already has another lead. Its Singapore base has identified the unknown craft, spotted landing somewhere in the Sea of Japan. And when in turn a

Soviet rocket disappeared in the middle of a launch, causing panic among navigators on the ground, the spacecraft that had captured it being undetectable because of radar jamming, the Americans at the Pentagon once again made a mistake in their analysis: "Forget Japan, we have combed the country, the hypothesis of a clandestine base in Japan does not hold water." American experts believe that the unknown rocket, which stole the Soviet shuttle, must have come down in the USSR. For its part, Great Britain has continued its investigations and is one step ahead of its American ally.

But true to his partnership across the Atlantic, as part of a general configuration of the free world alliance, Bond teams up with other figures in American espionage policy. Among the U.S. agents, he teams up with Holly Goodhead in *Moonraker*. An elite CIA spy and space engineering specialist, she is attached to NASA and works for the Space Research Administration. Goodhead has standard CIA equipment and uses effective defensive gadgets, such as the cyanide pen or the dart-equipped agenda. During an investigation in Venice, to find the *Moonraker* shuttle, which disappeared in mid-air and was transported by a Boeing 747, Bond suggested to Goodhead that they work together: "It's time to join forces," he told him, "Relaxation? Agreement? Cooperation? Trust?"

James Bond also proposes to Pola Ivanova, a spy member of the KGB, to join forces with other secret services to fight a common enemy. Bond met the Soviet agent in London, when she was touring the West with the Bolshoi ballet company. 007

met her again on a mission to San Francisco in *Dangerously Yours*: "Why do you think I sent you three dozen red roses?", Bond asked Ivanova, as they chose to listen to Tchaikovsky's music, to seal their reunion. The Russian replies, "Relaxation can be beautiful."

The geopolitical and friendly complicity between London and Moscow is frequent, reinforced during missions that promote strategic cooperation, as in *The Spy Who Loved Me*: at the same time disappear the Soviet submarine *Potemkin* and the British submarine *Ranger*, in possession on board of sixteen Polaris nuclear missiles. The First Lord of the Admiralty, Admiral Hargreaves, Commander-in-Chief of the Royal Navy, and Frederick Gray, the Minister of Defense, summon 007. In the Kremlin, in his office with the large red curtains, where one distinguishes a portrait of Lenin, the comrade general Alexis Gogol, head of the KGB, calls the agent Triple X. When Western and Russian defensive strategies are threatened, a common front is needed.

Commander James Bond of MI6 and Major Anya Amasova of the KGB join forces against the plans of Karl Stromberg, a wealthy Western capitalist. The businessman owns the *Liparus*, the largest tanker in the world. Thanks to a sophisticated submarine detection system, his tanker was able to seize British and Soviet submersibles. For what purpose?" I'm not interested in blackmail, I want to change the course of history by creating a new underwater world," Stromberg announced in front of the mural reproduction of Botticelli's

The Birth of Venus in his underwater city Atlantis, built to see out of time and space the ocean floor through the portholes, like the passengers in Captain Nemo's *Nautilus*. If this Jules Verne character is in search of another world, Stromberg, on the other hand, wishes for its destruction: "The present civilization will destroy itself, I am only accelerating the process. Observe my instruments of the apocalypse!" To stop him, Bond and Amasova cooperate together.

By the time they first meet, at the Mujaba Club bar in Cairo, they already know everything about each other: Bond chooses a Bacardi cocktail on the rocks for Agent Triple X, while Amasova asks the bartender for a vodka Martini mixed with a shaker and not a spoon for 007. Then, in order to make contact with the enemy, Bond and Amasova form a couple of oceanographer biologists, the Sterlings, who together enjoy the rental of an island cottage and a carriage ride along the Mediterranean. At another point, Bond and Amasova are summoned to a joint briefing, attended by Q, whose real name is Major Boothroyd, a specialist in gadgets and modern technology, and General Gogol of the KGB, later transferred in *Killing is not Playing* to Foreign Affairs and replaced by General Leonid Pushkin in the same position. Gogol and Pushkin immediately evoke Alexander Pushkin and Nicholas Gogol, immense poets and novelists, Russian by the way, and not Soviet. During this Anglo-Soviet meeting, 007 and Triple X oppose each other on the exact location of the underwater research laboratory: near which island did Stromberg install his secret base? Corsica for one, Sardinia for the other. This verbal joust of spies - who will have the last word - makes Gogol say, all smiles, that the two secret agents are made to cooperate and work together.

Such is, in fact, the geopolitical secret of 007's adventures: at the heart of the classic narrative of the secret services, James Bond is an exception in the field of espionage. He is the only national secret agent capable, in the middle of the Cold War, of leaving his strategic interests aside, the Western and anti-Soviet protection, to oppose a global and common enemy threatening to destroy the whole civilian population. But what does this singular rapprochement between James Bond and the USSR mean? Would he be a kind of double agent in the service of the Kremlin?

Outsider without borders

From this point of view, 007 assumes the role of outsider. His singularity places him beyond the stakes of the Cold War: he transcends the limits of the political conflict, goes beyond the classical opposition between Moscow and Washington, even makes the ideologies of the East and the West obsolete and useless.

Between the ethics of heroism and the principle of loyalty, James Bond develops a cross-border societal action of espionage. His political imagination renews pacts and stratagems.

His intuitive talent in the service of a democratic and humanist cause, without particular or national interests, gives his action a global influence and an international dimension.

Embodying diplomatic plasticity and strategic deterritorialization, Bond defends the citizens of each national identity, in the face of superpowered enemies bent on destroying society and heritage, economy and culture, history and human life.

The strength of the James Bond saga is that it does not reduce 007's adversary to the traditional enemies of the free world, which, after the Second World War, were the Soviet or Russian secret services: Cheka, Guepeu, NKVD, KGB, SMERSH (whose motto is *smiert spionom*, "death to spies") or FSB.

Against the Manichean dualism or binary political dichotomy, Kremlin versus Pentagon, Great Britain alone sets in motion a dialectic of rupture and continuity, in the face of dangerous adversaries whose post-national and post-political ambition is to endanger the entire planet.

The real enemies of 007 are not directly the Soviets, but dissidents of the USSR, fanatical military men or cruel despots promoting violence and hatred. Thus general Orlov in *Octopussy*. During a meeting in 1982 in Moscow on mutual disarmament with NATO, two voices oppose each other: that of Brezhnev and that of General Orlov. On the one hand, Leonid Brezhnev, the General Secretary of the Communist Party of the Soviet Union, relied on General Gogol's report, which called for stability, openness and dialogue with NATO, heralding the reformism of Mikhail Gorbachev, advocate of *glasnost* ("freedom of transparency") and *perestroika* ("reconstruction"). In *Octopussy*, Brezhnev declared: "The conversion of the world to socialism will be peaceful. Our military role is strictly defensive. Conversely, opposite him, General Orlov deploys on a giant screen, thanks to digital and computer Kutuzov, a virtual simulation of attack on Western Europe by the forces of the Warsaw Pact. Symbolizing the military offensive and the armed deployment of the State, he proposed to command thirty-one armored divisions in East Germany, five in Czechoslovakia and sixty on the western edge of the USSR. The Politburo strongly opposed.

In this new collaborative mission, MI6 and the KGB will work together. On the one hand, James Bond and his allies, Vijay of Universal Exports in New Delhi and Octopussy, daughter of Commander Dexter Smythe, and on the other hand, General Gogol and the East German soldiers. Together, they will try to stop General Orlov, associated with the bloodthirsty prince Kamal Kahn: the latter's plan is to detonate a nuclear bomb on the American base of Feldstadt, in West Germany, during a performance of Octopussy's circus. The end of the mission ends with a new Anglo-Soviet friendship: in order to maintain good international relations, the British government commits to hand over the Romanov Star to the USSR. Stolen by the traitor Orlov, this legendary sapphire is of inestimable value for the Russian cultural heritage.

The KGB becomes a recurring ally of 007. As early as 1962, when the Berlin Wall was being built and the world was being divided into two camps, James Bond was already anticipating the radical change to come in November 1989, the fall of the Wall and then the collapse of Soviet power in August 1991. James Bond's main and true enemy is not the camp opposite the one to which Great Britain belongs, but the enemy of all peoples: international conspiracy and global terrorism. This adversary has many faces. In *Casino Royale* and *Quantum of Solace*, Quantum is an international criminal organization, infiltrated in many Western countries, which makes profit by destabilizing democracies and supporting extremism and dictatorships. Another criminal organization goes by the name of "Spectre". Faced with this international syndicate of organized crime, which gives its name to the twenty-fourth film of the saga in 2015 soberly entitled *Spectre*, the scope of the action of the British secret agent 007 takes on a metaphysical scope and dimension.

The confrontation between Bond and the Spectre organization is a fight between good and evil, like the pre-credits or opening scene of *Spectre* in which Bond is plunged into the heart of the Day of the Dead in Mexico City. A combination of celebration and murder, of lightness and gravity, of life and death. If Bond has already investigated in Mexico City, in *Permit to Kill, Spectre* plunges him into a crowd with magnificent costumes, in full celebration, typical of the paintings of the Mexican artist José Guadalupe Posada, author of

La Catrina and other representations of death. *Spectre* shows here the duel between death and life, a duel relayed by the costumes, the dance and the music.

The Spectre organization made its appearance in the saga in 1962. Faced with Julius No, James Bond learns the true nature of his opponent. "So you work for the East," 007 asks him. "The East and the West are equal in their stupidity," replies Doctor No. At that moment, Bond learns the name of his enemy, with an expression mixed with fury and anguish. "I belong to the Spectre," Doctor No continues, expanding on the acronym, "Private Society of States Combining Terrorism, Revenge and Extortion. Smart criminal masterminds." The former treasurer of a Chinese secret society then explains that he has put his scientific knowledge, in nuclear matters and in radioactivity expertise, at the service of a criminal organization that Bond regularly confronts in the name of common human values of solidarity, justice and freedom.

To avenge the death of Doctor No, the Czechoslovakian chess champion Tov Kronsteen, number 5 of the Spectre, and the former operational head of the Smersh, Colonel Rosa Klebb, number 3, prepare a new international plot. Their primary objective is to seize the Lektor decoder, a computer with punched card information decryption chips. Beyond technological possession, Spectrum's real targets are the Russians and the British. The objective of the criminal organization is to reactivate the tensions between the two countries, in the heart of the Balkans.

The Spectrum is a global organization, as *Operation Thunderbolt* shows.

Some agents, like Emilio Largo, have a sign of recognition: a signet ring bearing the effigy of an octopus, an animal symbol that acts alone (the head of the animal) or in groups (its eight tentacles). Exploiting the fears of democratic governments, exacerbating international rivalries, threatening civilian populations, seeking to seize technological, economic or military knowledge, this association of specialists in counter-espionage, acts of violence, reprisals and extortion, has taken up residence in Paris. In a Haussmannian building, a few steps from the Champs-Élysées. When Spectre's number 2 parked near the building, he was immediately greeted by the French police. The Spectre's cover is indeed ideal. The organization hides behind a humanitarian and philanthropic aid organization, in the heart of the International Center for Displaced Persons. Behind the benevolence and welcome of the first offices, a diabolical organization is hidden. Once the metal curtain is closed, the meeting begins with an account of the operations in progress: extortion, kidnapping, racketeering, blackmail or political pressure, such as the assassination of a physicist who had gone to the East, which brought in three million francs paid by the Quai d'Orsay. Each Spectrum agent reports on his or her activities: the sale of Chinese drugs to the United States (number 11), the theft of the mail train (number 5), the blackmail of the Japanese double agent Fujiwa (number 7). Then the discussion stops.

Number 1 speaks up. We do not see his face, we do not know his name. Only his hand caressing a white Turkish angora cat is perceptible, through the partition that separates him from the rest of the assembly. His voice is slow and steady: "The Spectrum is a brotherhood whose strength lies in integrity." He then points to agents number 9 and 11, accusing one of them of betraying and defrauding the Spectrum. "I know the culprit, he will be punished," he says, triggering a deadly electric current at the same time. Unperturbed by the scene that has just taken place before his eyes, the number 2 of the Spectre calmly explains his plan.

At the top of the Spectre criminal organization, which sows death using the most diverse weapons of destruction (bacteriological virus, atomic bomb theft, space shuttle hijacking, geopolitical destabilization, organized crime), there is Ernst Stavro Blofeld, the number 1, alias Count Balthazar de Bleuchamp in *Her Majesty's Secret Service*, who uses cosmetic surgery and plastic transformation to change his face in *Diamonds are Forever*. It is he who makes Spectre the most important criminal organization. In the same film, *Her Majesty's Secret Service*, Bond meets Marc-Ange Draco, the head of the Corsican Union. The head of a mafia organization, whose activities are concealed by front companies (construction, electrical equipment, agricultural land), presents himself, with pride, as the leader of the largest international crime syndicate. 007 replies that "Spectre remains the most important of all".

All the criminal projects of the number 1, whose excessiveness exceeds the opposition of nations, make Bond the only international agent able to thwart them, in the service of the citizens of humanity. All but one, the most personal and cruel perhaps. It is on the orders of Blofeld, who drives the car from which a gunman machine-guns the couple, that James Bond's wife is murdered. Teresa Bond dies in her husband's arms, on the ledge of a sunny cliff, near the sea: "It's nothing, everything is fine, she is resting. We'll be leaving soon," Bond replies to the policeman on his motorcycle, alerted by the gunshots. 007 then takes Teresa's hand, with her wedding ring on her finger: "There's no hurry, we have eternity ahead of us." Then Bond kisses her hands, then her face, behind the bride's veil, which now hides them both and brings them closer for eternity. A moment later, a bird lands beside them. This final monologue, probably the most moving of the entire saga, seals death and love in the same tragic and ancient scene: James Bond cries.

Ersnt Stavro Blofeld is the worst criminal the British agent has ever faced.

Thus, we must distinguish between aesthetics and politics. On the one hand, in the work of James Bond, the visual and narrative aesthetics evolve in three stages: the Hitchcockian classicism of the sixties embodied by *Goodbye Russia*, then the adventure style of the eighties where epic and fantasy coexist, like *Moonraker*, after the pop and psychedelic attempt of *Her Majesty's Secret Service*. Finally, the return to the realism and dark symbolism of espionage, like *Skyfall* in 2012 or *Spectre* in 2015.

On the other hand, if James Bond's work is appreciated by spectators all over the world, it is due to the fact that its political dimension, on the screen, soothes the strategic balance and softens the real diplomatic chessboard, in reality. Between fiction and reality, two political facts are here to be put in resonance, in order to underline the gap: in February 1984, under the pretext of defending the interests of the United States, the American president Roland Reagan supports the CIA and engages in a secret war in Nicaragua, by parachuting military troops against the socialist Sandinista government, "seed of the evil" according to Reagan. This terrible conflict caused many victims. And the Hollywood cinema of this period is impregnated with the trauma of the war and the violence of the fights, as illustrated, in 1983, about another war, the film *Rambo, first blood*. On its side, the cinema of 007 also reacts, in its own way, by seeking appeasement. A few months later, in May 1985, in *Dangerously Yours*, James Bond receives the medal of the Order of Lenin from the hands of General Gogol, who has become his friend in the course of cooperation missions. The boss of the KGB toasts the award with the British Minister of Defense and points out that it is the first time it is given to a foreigner.

James Bond understood this and explained it to the world's leaders: between diplomats and gentlemen, it is better to settle political disputes in a casino, around a gambling table, than on a battlefield, in the middle of a war. As *the* scene of the race on the Olympic track between the GDR skier Erich Kriegler and his West German opponent Hans Wolf shows, the competition between the great powers is no longer military - *hard power* - but playful and sporting - *soft power*. Beyond East and West, *game save the Queen*. Such is the political secret of 007.

2. Between Britishness and globality, the creation of chaos-cinema

*"Mr. Bond, you have what
the Greeks call* thrassos.
Milos Colombo to 007,
For your eyes only

A symbol of Anglicity and the embodiment of Britishness, James Bond is the perfect agent in the service of the Great Albion, named after the mythological giant, son of Poseidon and brother of Atlas. But beyond his national integrity, isn't the hero of the spy services also a citizen of the world, sensitive to the hybrid effects of globality and the plural transformation of cultures? Between cosmopolitanism and multiculturalism, the 007 films constitute a laboratory that questions the notion of identity subject to multiple metamorphoses. Would James Bond be a plural being?

Trip to the UK

The personification of integrity and loyalty, James Bond is the symbol of commitment to the service of the Crown. Nothing seems to keep him from the right path: defending his country, protecting the Queen's interests, wearing the colors of the Empire. The secret agent 007 is the figure par excellence of Britishness. While MI6's official cover is the London-based Universal Exports, Bond is the ideal representative of this buying and selling company: as a secret agent, he exports Britain's cultural samples to the world. He is like the product he has to sell and promotes and advertises it in each of his adventures.

At the heart of the action, Bond constantly reminds us of the anglicity that underlies it. It is this that commands his missions and imposes an imperative of success. To fail would be to fail England.

All the referential ingredients of the British culture are thus gathered in the films. They are the symbols of the country, as well as the secret services. The Bank of England, the media of the British Broadcasting Corporation (BBC), the bell of Big Ben, the Elizabeth clock tower of the Parliament, the river Thames, where there is a crazy chase between the black boat of Bond and the white boat of his adversary in *The World Is Not Enough*. The films also show the London Underground, Westminster Bridge, Trafalgar Square, Piccadilly Circus, double-decker buses, bobbies with round helmets or the

British Museum, founded in 1753, which is located at the intersection of Bloomsbury, Covent Garden and Oxford Street. There are also the London cabs, nicknamed "black cabs", like the one driven by an MI6 agent who is signaled by 007 in *Octopussy to* follow Prince Kamal Khan to Heathrow Airport, after the auction of Carl Fabergé's green and gold imperial Easter egg at Sotheby's, on the aptly named Bond Street. This street refers to the name of Baronet Thomas Bond, a distant ancestor of James. Combining art stores, antique stores and high fashion boutiques, London's Bond Street, located in the historic heart of Mayfair, has attracted many poets and artists throughout the ages, such as the engraver Gustave Doré. In the saga of 007, we also find the red telephone box, typical of the capital, also called "aquarium" - typical of the urban furniture of London. This well-known iconographic sign has been installed in the English streets since 1921, on the initiative of the General Post Office.

Other elements of British culture appear outside the city of London, such as the famous British transatlantic liner *Queen Elizabeth*, a symbol of luxury and Art Deco, which sank in 1972 in Hong Kong's Victoria Harbour, and which serves as a secret hideout for MI6 HQ in *The Man with the Golden Gun*. The wreck of the ship remains tilted in the bay. The floors are leaning, but usable, and the boat allows the British spies some peace and quiet, out of sight of the American and Chinese secret services. James Bond meets up with M, Q, Lieutenant Hip and Professor Frazier. Together they review the Sol-X, a solar-powered device capable of converting solar energy into radio electricity. The investigation of Francisco Scaramanga then becomes clearer on board the *Queen Elizabeth*.

So many scenes, objects, monuments and landscapes that are worth signing.

As a British subject, James Bond discovers his personal lineage by learning more about his historical ancestry. In the cinema, on the screen, the spectator shares the family and cultural recognition of 007. During a mission where he has to learn the science of genealogy, in order to make his cover credible, he is initiated on his own origins by a renowned specialist of the Heraldic Office. Sir Hilary Bray tells James Bond that he has found the knightly arms of his ancestors. The arms of Sir Thomas Bond, Baronet of Peckham, who died in 1734, consist of three bezants Argent and a chevron Sable. The Latin motto on his family crest is *Orbis non sufficit,* "The world is not enough." Going further back in genealogy, James Bond is related to Otho the Good, who received the fief of Wickhambreaux from the Count of Thanet in 1387. Bond's family comes from the locality in the county of Kent.

This intimate connection to the English countryside of Kent, located southeast of London between the English Channel and the Thames Estuary, further strengthens Bond's attachment to the Crown.

In various situations, James Bond shows a certain attraction to patriotic sentiment. In philosophically significant scenes, he regularly shows this loyalty. *Rule, Britannia!*.

After returning from Jamaica at the beginning of *Goodbye Russia*, Bond whistles his way to MI6 headquarters. He enters to the tune of *For he's a jolly good fellow*, an English adaptation of the popular French song *Malbrough s'en va-t-en guerre*. This eighteenth-century tune evokes the 1709 battle of Malplaquet between the French led by Marshal de Villars and the Austrian and Dutch forces led by the Duke of Marlborough, John Churchill. According to the patriotic variations of the song, each protagonist of the conflict interprets differently the outcome of the battle, won by the anti-French coalition, but at the cost of a heavy sacrifice of human lives. The Duke of Marlborough, who was only wounded during this battle, is announced as dead in the French version of the song. In good spirits when he arrives at MI6, James Bond seems to appreciate this patriotic musical tune. He respects its codes and values.

Shortly afterwards, at the end of the mission that took him to the heart of the Balkans, James Bond and Corporal Tatiana Romanova are in Venice. The two agents posed as a married couple, Caroline and David Somerset, a discreet cover for their train journey between Sofia, Belgrade, Zagreb and Trieste. Looking at the ring that had been used for their fake union, and which was no longer of any use, the spy of the Soviet Smersh security services asked the British agent: "Can I keep the ring? This ring can be used again. Bond replies, "What belongs to the state belongs to the state." Bond does not deviate from his political role here. His speech embodies administrative righteousness and legal legality: the investment of government services and the national interest of public finances must be respected. The law is binding on every citizen, Bond seems to suggest, recalling, in his own way, the motto "God and my right", the political motto of the Royal Arms of the United Kingdom, written in French in the official version.

Whether he is tortured or seduced, loving or violent, submissive or willing, James Bond serves his country.

Both solitary and supportive, he puts his individual qualities at the service of the British national collective. In *Operation Thunderbolt, Bond* confronts Fiona Volpe, the head of the Spectre's Enforcement Branch, an outstanding driver, a top-notch markswoman and a femme fatale, and is captured by her. For 007, there is no possible relationship from confrontation to seduction, from confrontation to association, from alliance to pact, except in service to the nation. Personal desire is excluded from the order of the mission whose outcome can only be for the benefit of England. "I acted only to serve my country", he launches then, in challenge to the redoubtable ally of Émilio Largo.

Faced with Helga Brandt, number 11 of the Spectre, in *On ne vit que deux fois,* he poses as an industrial spy specializing in chemical processes. During his interrogation, Bond is easy prey for the woman who is trying to extract a confession from him by any means necessary. Without revealing his true identity, Bond agrees to be seduced. Faced with his adversary, he replies, "What wouldn't I do for England?"

England is present everywhere in the James Bond series, and the spy never leaves England during his travels around the world.

In *Diamonds Are Forever,* for example, everyone, CIA or MI6, is looking for a small cassette case, from South Africa to Amsterdam, from Las Vegas, Nevada to Baja, California. On this box is a picture of the *World's* Greatest Marches. This coded tape allows Ernst Stavro Blofeld, number 1 of the Spectrum, to control the diamond laser satellite launched into orbit to threaten international civil security. The image of the tape represents one of the symbols of England, since one clearly distinguishes the British guard of Buckingham Palace in ceremonial dress. The guards are wearing the traditional patriotic costume of the Windsor ceremony, in particular the black textured helmeted cap with a feather plume. Bond's goal is to retrieve this tape, but one might think that he is doing so as much to save the world as to preserve the integrity of an image symbolic of the culture across the Channel. It is this image that everyone in the film is after.

During a mission in the Austrian Alps, near Berngarten, in the opening of *The Spy Who Loved Me*, Bond stays in a mountain chalet. There he receives a message in the form of a magnetic strip on his connected watch. In the message, M asks him to return to headquarters immediately. Obliged to leave the Swiss mountains, Bond does not hesitate to say a quick goodbye to the one who is accompanying him at the time. "James, I need you," she tells him, in order to hold back her lover for a moment. 007 replies immediately, because he has already made his choice: "England too. Again in *The Spy Who Loved Me*, this time facing the Soviet agent Anya Amasova, a temporary partner and momentary ally on this mission, Bond utters the following sentence, significant of his sincere and recurring commitment: "I score for Britain."

After a jump in the air, equipped only with a harness and a grappling hook, at the top of a huge dam, Bond infiltrates a chemical weapons factory in Arkhangelsk, in the north of Russia, four years after the collapse of the USSR, in the opening of the film *GoldenEye*. 007 meets 006 there. "For England, James?", asks the latter. "For England, Alec!", confirms him with determination the spy.

Not only does Bond seem to claim the British political order, but he also shows signs of it: in the middle of the missions, where his life depends on his discretion, where the revelation of his British identity could threaten his existence at any moment, Bond does not hesitate to take out the flag, the standard of the coming victory.

Created in 1606, after the union of the Crowns, the Union Jack brings together different emblems and several colors in a single figure: the cross of St. George of England, the cross of St. Andrew of Scotland, then later, the Union Flag increases the cross of St. Patrick representing Ireland. In front of his enemies, James Bond mobilizes the flag and takes out the Union Jack. As a sign of defiance or provocation? As a sign of triumph or superiority? But perhaps it is simply the desire to support the nation in all circumstances and to show, once again, his attachment to his country.

Like a soccer fan, delighted to support his national club team, Bond shows the colors of the British flag on various occasions. The secret mission is actually an opportunity to show his national support and to salute the flag of his country's fan club: leaving the enemies who are pursuing him far behind, the hero opens a large parachute in the colors of the Union Jack during a ski jump over a cliff, in *The Spy Who Loved Me*. On another occasion, he unfurls the United Kingdom's Union Flag on the canvas of a hot air balloon for a trip over New Delhi to attack Kamal Khan's Monsoon Palace in *Octopussy*. Elsewhere, when he opens the hatch of a submarine disguised as an iceberg on the ice floe, the hatch bears the colors of the Union Jack, in *Dangerously Yours*.

A supranational icon, James Bond agrees to play the role of flag bearer for the British delegation.

Here, the intelligence and infiltration professional refuses concealment and rejects discretion. Doesn't he need cover or camouflage techniques to preserve his identity? Yet they are so essential to the survival of a secret agent. As the key to successful missions, false identities are the key to staying alive in the heart of the enemy. But not for Bond. Out of the ordinary and far from the ordinary, he prefers to risk death by assuming his *made-in-England* status rather than having to hide his Britishness and his 100% *British* identity.

The taste of sherry

In 1952, when he began writing the first adventures of his hero, Ian Fleming also had all the characteristics of a perfect subject of Her Majesty. Winston Churchill had been a close friend of the family for a long time: Ian Fleming's father had died in battle at Ypres in May 1917. At the time of his death, Churchill himself wrote the eulogy in the *Times*.

Among his professional activities, Ian Fleming had several jobs, such as journalist or stockbroker, but he also worked for the United Kingdom's intelligence service. As a simple assistant and then as chief of staff, he collaborated with the secret service of the British Admiralty. It was in this context that he was entrusted with several delicate missions: Ian Fleming tried to set up two secret operations, *Enigma* in the Atlantic and *Goldeneye* in North Africa, which remained mere projects. But these missions, even if they were not carried out, were no less effective in terms of fiction: to create his hero, Fleming drew on his professional contacts and personal friendships.

To find out where James Bond's sense of patriotism comes from, we need only look at the secret agents and close friends of Fleming who inspired the creation of the hero.

First, the anti-communist and double agent Sidney Reilly. Thanks to his talent and courage, this accomplished spy gained the trust of Winston Churchill and Captain Mansfield Smith-Cumming, the founder of MI6. The British leaders considered Reilly to be a charismatic, daring and brilliant spy during his various missions. Ian Fleming met him on several occasions.

There is also the Canadian William Stephenson. A hero of military aviation, he was the founder of the British Security Coordination (BSC). At the request of Winston Churchill, this British intelligence service, in charge of missions on American soil, brought together more than three hundred agents with the aim of intercepting and listening to various coded messages. At the head of this team, William Stephenson was Churchill's master spy during the Second World War. He also has all the traits of a real James Bond.

There is another secret agent who also inspired Ian Fleming to create the character of James Bond, in the person of Patrick Dalzel-Job. He is a British naval officer and commander of submarine operations. Sometimes undisciplined and instinctive, like 007, Dalzel-Job has a personal sense of what he should and should not do. He decides himself to evacuate, against the order of his command, the civilian population of the port of Narvik, in Norway, a few days before its bombing by the German army. Patrick Dalzel-Job, a close friend of Ian Fleming's, was awarded the Knight's Cross of the Royal Norwegian Order of St. Olaf by the King of Norway, Haakon VII, in recognition of his action, which was certainly illegal.

Among these various real and authentic figures of Anglo-Saxon espionage, the one closest to 007 is undoubtedly the British agent of MI6, Wilfred Dunderdale. A member of the Royal Navy and another friend of Ian Fleming's, Wilfred

Dunderdale served as head of the Paris office of the Secret Intelligence Service in the 1930s. Fleming drew inspiration from his unusual and charismatic personality to create the style of 007.

Surrounded by real Anglo-Saxon secret agents, Ian Fleming did not fail to highlight the qualities of his spy friends in order to create the other characters, secondary or allied, in his saga: Fleming personally met Allen Dulles, the central director of American intelligence. There is a direct link between reality and fiction. Allen Dulles had all the traits of the character of Felix Leiter, a CIA agent, a recurring ally and a major figure in the adventures of the British hero. Other American agents, such as William J. Donovan, the director of the Office of Strategic Services (OSS), whom Fleming knew, also inspired the character of Leiter.

In order to find the characteristic traits of the authoritarian, sometimes fatherly, sometimes motherly figure of M, who embodies the head of the Intelligence Service, Fleming drew directly on his own superior, Admiral John Godfrey, in other words the director of the British Naval Intelligence Division. He also took on aspects of the personality of Officer Maxwell Knight. Initially recruited by the Makgill Agency, a private intelligence company, Maxwell Knight later became the head of the Infiltration Section of MI5 from 1931 to 1961, the British Domestic Intelligence Service.

If James Bond is the fictional hero of extraordinary adventures, his creator Ian Fleming gave him the realistic features of real Anglo-Saxon heroes, British or American agents of the Second World War.

Beyond the visual signs of British identity, such as the Union Jack flag, beyond the actual characters of secret agents in the service of Her Majesty who inspired him, such as Wilfred Dunderdale, James Bond masters to perfection the codes of his island culture.

James Bond has the tastes, features, gestures and attitudes of the perfect English gentleman.

With a sip in his mouth, James Bond can easily identify the vintage of a spirit that the British like so much: sherry, the historic Anglo-Saxon name for sherry, to which we owe our current name. It is in the company of M and Sir Donald Munger, in *Diamonds are Forever*, that 007 makes this demonstration: by tasting a glass of sherry, Bond immediately recognizes the year of the vinification process, 1851, as well as the manufacturing method from which this alcohol comes, the solera.

This philosophical example proves how perfectly Bond embodies the codes of the British subject: a symbol of refinement and distinction, the secret agent sublimates the aesthetic rules of London style. British wine has no secrets for him, especially the one that the English appreciate most.

Bond has his habits, and they are part of the British culture of his time. In his wallet, he has a membership card for the very private club "The Ambassadors' Circle" as well as for another club, equally private but more popular, even underground and clandestine, the Playboy Casino card. UK 40 401.

James Bond is faithful to the habits and customs that the English appreciate. First of all, he is attached to the tradition of *five o'clock tea*, a habit that dates back to 1662, at the time of the marriage between the English king Charles II and Catherine of Braganza. It is a national ritual, as Hugo Drax reminds his guest during their first short interview in *Moonraker*. While he has built a royal residence in California, every stone of which comes from France, the cruel Hugo Drax addresses James Bond, invited to his palace, first as a Briton: "You have arrived at the moment that coincides with your country's contribution to Western civilization, tea time. A cucumber sandwich?"

Determined by national cultural codes, James Bond follows conventions to the letter. Fixed in his being by traditional habits, and frozen in his existence by normative classicism, Bond makes ritual a personal and recognizable mark.

Everyone knows Bond's habits, his adversaries and allies alike. When the bloodthirsty South American drug cartel baron, Franz Sanchez, identifies James Bond in *Licence to Kill*, he immediately says to him, "A British agent, I knew it. You're a class act." Inside his bar in St. Petersburg in *GoldenEye*, former KGB agent Valentin Zukovsky gives a quick portrait of 007 in front of him, "James Bond, the secret agent as charming as he is refined." The Cossack Janus' rival then adds, with a laugh, "In a shaker, not with a spoon?" This is a reference, known to all, to one of the constant traits of the hero's personality, his taste for the vodka Martini cocktail, "shaken, but not stirred".

James Bond's personal blend follows a precise dosage: three measures of vodka, half a measure of dry vermouth, a twist of lemon. In *Killing is Not Playing*, for example, cellist Kara Milovy prepares 007's favorite cocktail in the room of the Île-de-France hotel in Tangier. "You remembered," James Bond says to her, moved, as she hands him her already prepared glass. "To us!" he says. "Na zdorovié!", replies the one who plays on a unique instrument, the Lady Rose, a Stradivarius of Cremona, instrument made as a rare piece in 1724. "Did I pass your cocktail?", asks, worried, the girlfriend of General Koskov. But James Bond barely has time to answer her, because, in a daze, he realizes that his drink has been drugged with chloral hydrate. The vodka Martini cocktail is such a sacred ritual that it even becomes a weakness here, which can betray or endanger the hero. If someone hands him his favorite cocktail with a smile, why should he be suspicious?

Faithful to his tastes, recognizable in his gestures, James Bond is a man of habit. He remains constant in what characterizes his singularity and founds his authenticity. The pleasure of rituals constitutes 007's identity. But to what extent? Reason of coherence and element of stability, such are the ingredients of his psychological and sociological state. The fidelity to the morals of the English education goes hand in hand, in his case, with a character based on the repetition of clean and identifiable features between all.

A recurring invariant, among others, a rule that has become a principle: British humor.

Humor, phlegm and detachment are also characteristics of the Anglo-Saxon spirit. James Bond regularly accompanies his distinction and elegance with a play on wit or a line of humor. Phlegmatism and detachment are Anglo-Saxon characteristics that the spy wears at every opportunity. Also called *nonsense*, British humor is linked to absurdity, eccentricity and provocation. It stages characters or situations and then makes fun of them.

James Bond has a sophisticated taste for sarcasm. In *Goldfinger*, when he first hears the name Auric Goldfinger uttered by his friend Felix Leiter, Bond laughs: "Is that a Parisian nail polish?" Elsewhere, in *Operation Thunderball*, Bond is summoned to work on the confidential *Thunderball* file that bears the top secret inscription "Not to be opened until officially authorised." In the middle of a crisis cell, Miss Moneypenny warns him: "In the big meeting room, things are heating up, all the 00s from Europe are there, along with the Minister of the Interior." But Bond keeps his sense of humour. He prefers to mock and ironize: "His wife has lost their dog? Sometimes humor becomes political denigration and derision. Without lacking truth or seriousness in his judgement, Bond can only see the turmoil of the world with distance and derision. The arcana of international politics is just a game he is playing. In *GoldenEye*, in 1995, Bond ironizes in front of M about the alleged new-found freedom of the peoples. 007 measures the cynicism of Realpolitik and is under no illusion about the recent democratic overthrow of former totalitarian regimes. He tells M: "Governments change, not lies."

Refined and distinguished, Bond also wields irony and humor as weapons of defense. He deploys the outward signs of the British elite - patriotic loyalty, a taste for service - and adds his own personal trait and singular quirkiness: a form of disobedience, a confidence in instinct, with a touch of sarcasm and a zest for provocation. Insubordinate and insubordinate in appearance, loyal and constant in depth, such is Bond's non-conformism set up as a rule of life.

Bond has a British respect for convention, as evidenced by the elegance of his suit as he arrives at the office, but he throws his hat at the entrance to Universal Exports Ltd, the company that serves as MI6's cover. He signals his arrival with a mixture of defiant casualness and respectful classicism.

As the perfect embodiment of the British subject, the spy is both the model and the copy, the standard and the reproduction. He embodies the repetitive *replay*. This is why, sometimes, in the middle of his adventures, 007 seems almost unmotivated or slightly nonchalant.

James Bond can then give the impression of being crossed by the ancient notion of *akèdia*, which means "lack of interest". Between detachment and casualness, does the secret agent suffer from a repetition complex? Does he see his existence as a tireless routine and eternal repetition of the same actions? From mission to mission, the Sisyphus of spies faces the same adventures, to prove the intact greatness of Great Britain.

Faced with these identical situations, he must maintain moral integrity and effective obstinacy. True to his unchanging identity, his tastes and inclinations are stable. Yet his adventures seem so extraordinary to us, so why should he get tired? But despite being the exact opposite of routine everydayness and ordinary banality, 007's exploits base their narrative on repetition.

So, in the ceaseless rhythm of spectacular actions, could Bond be trapped in solitude, wanting to escape from boredom and feeling seized by melancholy? Could the overflow of adventures eventually become monotonous, dull and mechanical? Sometimes the language of espionage becomes empty, disembodied and worn out, as it is not renewed. Touched by spleen, James Bond becomes an almost bovarian hero.

The crossing of the repetitions, within the framework of its extraordinary professional activity, produces in 007 a certain monotony. Britishness, as a transparent and recurrent grid of cultural codes, is partly responsible for the melancholic greyness of the spy. Anglicity, a normative cultural standard, brings Her Majesty's agent into an empty seriality. Defined by coded signifiers, marked by internal aesthetic and narrative criteria, the spy then feels the need to get rid of them. It is time for James Bond to metamorphose.

Breathless

Worn-out body and tired mind, James Bond is out of breath. He regularly needs to rest, as in *Operation Thunder*, when 007 is sent to a medical clinic in the south of England, after his violent confrontation with the Spectre's number 6, Colonel Jacques Bouvard. Wounded in the shoulder in *The World Is Not Enough*, wounded again in *Skyfall*, now vulnerable, fragile and tormented, 007 gets older. He becomes, little by little, a victim of his own identity, which he carries like a weight, and can have tendencies to self-destruction. If he starts to doubt his capacities, it is because his loss of breath is much more than a simple physical accident : is he worn out by the repetition of his missions, tired of the similarity of his exploits which follow one another indefinitely, indistinctly ?

The adventure of secrecy, which leads Bond to intervene to save the country from the threat, becomes a metaphysical quest on the meaning of existence, where his own identity is at stake. The questioning of oneself produces an ontological electroshock. In other words, the model of Britishness, carried by 007 in a constant and permanent way, begins to mark signs of crack and fragmentation. The identity of the self, that of a charismatic hero in the service of the free world, is in crisis.

James Bond will break with the permanence of his identity to enter the contingency of the world and undergo the transformations of reality.

In a violent, precarious and unstable universe, subject to destruction, threatened by unscrupulous beings, Bond's raw existence is also dominated by experience and carried by the vagaries.

The hero expresses the singular condition of solitude; driven by an individual destiny, he constantly puts his action and his freedom at stake. An existential and social castaway, James Bond resembles the heroes of Joyce, Faulkner or Sartre, who are distraught and lost.

Faced with pure ideals, James Bond can only trust his raw existence, his destiny here and now. Nothing else matters but the present situation, the actuality of reality at a given moment. Surrounded by a political bestiary and facing faceless enemies, 007 sees a world populated by individuals devoid of consciousness. All his being is concentrated in this state of presence, in permanent connection with what surrounds him.

Existential character, the secret agent is crossed by the contingency of reality. The test of existence leads the hero to grasp the world as it is - a world in movement -, and to break with stability. How should he react? What should he do in the face of the unexpected and upheavals? 007 must grasp himself as an individual in a situation, subject to the vagaries of the world. Bond does not remain prisoner of the stability, full and whole, of the being. On the contrary, he enters into the becoming of the being. He transforms himself, undergoes upheavals and shocks, reacts to the phenomena encountered. Of British subject frozen in its being, Bond enters the becoming of the world and takes part then in the metamorphosis. What happens in the character's consciousness? Caught up in the vertigo of freedom and the authenticity of solitude, the Bondian hero grasps himself as lacking in the world. Carried by the desire to disengage himself and by the responsibility to assume himself, he surpasses himself to build himself differently.

The three metamorphoses

To the reproduction of the same, to the return of the identical and to the mimetic repetition, are opposed here the trembling, the hybridity and the crossbreeding.

How does the spy react to events and circumstances? He adapts and transforms himself. Carried along by the movement of the world, open to reality in all its diversity and singularity, Bond never remains the same; he changes his being according to the situation. This is how it is in *On ne vit que deux fois*, a film about metamorphosis and transformation.

The fluidity of the hero is expressed in the opening scene: when Bond leaves on a mission to Tokyo, Miss Moneypenny of MI6 hands him a book of linguistic rudiments to learn the basics of the Japanese language in no time, but Bond declines. He doesn't need it because, as a citizen of the world, 007 has a degree in Oriental languages from Cambridge University. In the same film, when he meets Henderson, his first contact on the spot, the latter has been living in Tokyo for twenty-eight years and wears a traditional Japanese kimono. He explains to Bond that, despite many years living in the country, it is very difficult to assimilate the local culture. However, Bond immediately impresses him by telling him the ideal temperature for drinking hot *ginjo* or *daiginjo* sake, namely forty degrees or *nurukan*. Surprised, Henderson congratulates Bond for this expertise, which is very rare among westerners. Tigre Tanaka, the head of the Japanese secret service, had the same reaction, praising Bond's knowledge of Japanese culture: "Remarkable subtlety, for a European. Further on, Bond is even able to quote a Japanese proverb by heart: "Never will the bird make its nest on a bare tree."

But the real transformation takes place a little later in the film. It is about Bond's three metamorphoses: becoming Japanese, becoming a ninja, becoming a husband.

To infiltrate the small island of Matsu, halfway between Kobe and Shanghai, and investigate a mysterious volcanic crater in the heart of the archipelago of four thousand islands, Bond undergoes a metamorphosis. From being a simple British subject, he opens himself up to different forms of otherness: the language of the other, the culture of the other, the habits and customs beyond the borders. A hybridization of the self, sensitive, decentered and multiple. Bond differs from himself, in a gesture of uprooting and dissemination. The *difference* is thought in the gap and is lived in the incompletion. Identity is not given: it is to come, it is a construction and a journey. While he is a British subject, is Bond becoming a postcolonial citizen?

The first metamorphosis takes place in a Japanese palace, surrounded by trees and flowers, and offers to Bond an aestheticization of the body. In order to change his being, duplicity and self-duplication are achieved by altering his external features and physical appearance. 007 lies on a table in an operating room with glittering windows. One surrounds him and one shaves him the hairs of the chest. Before putting on a golden kimono, his body, his hair and his eyebrows are transformed. Like a being in suspension, he becomes momentarily Japanese and leaves his British identity. It is a physical and corporal metamorphosis.

The second metamorphosis is athletic and mental. To improve his reflexes and powers of concentration, the British agent undergoes training in modern ninja combat techniques, subjected to intense exercises by Tigre Tanaka. For several days, at the top of the Japanese mountains, in the middle of nature, Bond abandons the western sophistication of Q's gadgets to discover the electronic and digital arsenal of the ninjas, associated with traditional combat weapons, such as the *sansatukan shureido*, the *shuriken* or the *shaken*. It is a metamorphosis linked to the strength of the spirit and mental wisdom. Japan offers Bond the alliance of nature (the physical strength of the ninja, the raw body) and technology (robotic innovations, the sophistication of gadgets).

Finally, Bond's third metamorphosis is cultural and sentimental. In traditional dress, Bond goes to a temple where three simultaneous weddings are being celebrated. The ceremonial is strict, as is the matrimonial protocol. The man, on the one hand, walks towards the temple, where his wife is waiting for him, whom he discovers and meets at that very moment. As part of the ceremony, Bond then marries Kissy Suzuki, a Japanese intelligence agent who operates as an ama diver. Even though the wedding is a secret cover, it takes place in front of the bride's family, surrounded by her relatives and friends, and following religious rules: prayer reading, singing, purification ritual. At the end of the union, the husband and wife hold out their hands together to drink the sacred water. It is a spiritual and cultural metamorphosis.

The fulfillment of the three metamorphoses is completed when Bond becomes a laborer and fisherman, moving to the island where he settles with his wife. Transformed, he drives a humble fisherman's boat, wears simple, light-colored clothes, a straw hat and a scarf. Anonymous among the fish sellers, he settles on the fishermen's island, in a modest house, with his benevolent wife. This honeymoon following the wedding is, of course, a cover for the secret agent, because, at the same time, danger is felt and the international crisis is near: the United States warns the USSR of the imminent takeoff of an American rocket that, if hijacked, would cause an escalation of tensions between the two blocks. Meanwhile, while Tanaka's ninjas explore the island without success, a young girl from the fishing port discovers Ryusaki's cave, surrounded by a deadly gas, phosgene, which keeps visitors away. Bond and his wife decide to walk across the island for many hours to reach this remote spot. The spy, who is no longer quite the same, finally reaches the site of a bubbling lake, near a volcanic crater located away from the island area.

Sensitive to the desedimentation of the self, the anglicity and the Britishness leave place in Bond to the *kominka* or process of Japaneseization. Would the saga of the 007 films allow a meeting of cultures? Is Bond cosmopolitan, a vector for the development of diversity?

One of the most striking scenes, in the last part of *On ne vit que deux fois*, presents a situation that goes beyond the sole national perspective and explores an original polyglottism and linguistic decentering. This episode shows Bond in a transhistorical and transgeographical relationship to the world, as if the action opened onto a decentered and disrupted universe. The scene invites us to think about the unpredictable and the unexpected, about trembling and diffraction.

On the Japanese island of Kyushu, the luxurious control room of the secret base is decorated with paintings of great masters, especially Dutch and Italian. In this place resides the supreme leader of the international organization Spectre. From a Greek mother and a Polish father, Ernst Stavro Blofeld caresses his white angora cat, also called "Turkish angora". Then a confrontation takes place between, on the one hand, the British spy disguised as a Japanese and, on the other, Hans, the robust and imposing German bodyguard of the founder of the Spectre. At the end of the fight, Bond throws Hans into a bathtub infested with piranhas, predators of South American freshwater like Guyana and Colombia. Then, in a Scottish accent, James Bond declares, in French, "Bon appétit! This sentence, pronounced in French by a British agent with a Scottish accent, addressed to a German opponent, concludes a scene marked by polyglottism. Moreover, saying "Bon appétit!" in French is a habit with James Bond, who also repeats it in *Permit to Kill*: when he investigates Milton Krest's genetic laboratory at night about marine animals, especially sharks, Bond gets rid of a guard by wishing him "Bon appétit!"

So many indications of national cultures, certainly, but which meet and exchange in the same scene: Japan, Netherlands, Italy, Greece, Poland, Turkey, England, Germany, Guyana or Colombia, France and Scotland.

Would James Bond be not so much a British subject closed on his identity, but more a citizen of the world, open to differences and otherness?

The world is yours

The expression "citizen of the world" has several meanings and refers to the human condition on earth, to the cultivated and civilized being, or to the individual open to others. In the end, it refers to the open-mindedness of a person sensitive to all that humanity has in common, beyond singular customs and closed borders. Traveler and nomad, James Bond himself could embody this formula of cosmopolitanism, defined by Fougeret de Monbron in *Le Citoyen du monde* (1750): "Today I am in London, perhaps in six months I will be in Moscow, in Petersburg, what do I know? It would not be a miracle if I were one day in Ispahan or Peking.

Against the withdrawal and rooting in a land, a language or a culture, Bond participates in the exchange and the opening to other countries. Cosmopolitanism - which is not incompatible with a certain patriotic attachment, as is the case with James Bond - is especially opposed to nationalist ideology. If the global phenomenon of globalization is worrying, threatening to standardize our emotions and ways of functioning for the benefit of a vast liberal system, what answer can be given? Should society be rooted in an exclusive, local, linguistic or cultural identity in order to escape the laws of the market, or is it preferable to open up to creative crossings, to the hybridization of the world? Bond has chosen: he is a cosmopolitan - from the Greek *kosmopolitès*, "citizen" (*politès*) of the "world" (*kosmos*) - and, beyond the borders of his island, is open to others. The cosmopolitan spirit is opposed to world trade as well as to the nationalist spirit. James Bond, antidote to both identity-based *Brexit* and standardized globalization?

As an advocate of mutual enrichment and of a composite diversity of cultures, in crossing and sharing, Bond feels at ease in the places and spaces he crosses. Each region seems familiar and familiar to him. He succeeds in living in the world, without being a stranger anywhere and assimilating local customs and habits as if they were his own. In *Nothing But Your Eyes, for* example, James Bond is invited to dinner by the Greek businessman, Signor Aris Kristatos, at the casino on the island of Corfu. Bond is a fine gourmet and does not hesitate for a second in his choices among the local gastronomy. He knows better than anyone what to order for a fine dining experience: "I'll have the prawns of Prezera, a salad and the bourdetto", says Bond without hesitation. The region of Prezera is located in the northwest of Greece, at the mouth of the Ambracian Gulf, and bourdetto is a famous fish dish from Corfu. After this composition announced by Bond, Kristatos, claiming the culture of his country and wishing to show that he, himself, is the true connoisseur, says to the secret agent: "May I suggest a white robola from Kefalonia, my native region?" Bond, who could hardly refuse this culinary advice, went on to make another suggestion: "Forgive me, but I find this wine too fragrant. I prefer Theotaki Aspro. 007 has a culture as precise and detailed as his Greek host, because the Theotaki Aspro is the name of a white wine produced by a prestigious wine producer of Corfu. So he was right in his choice.

As an experimental laboratory for the porosity of borders, the Bond saga questions the interdependence of cultures, their difference, their singularity and their complementarity. In what sense is James Bond cosmopolitan? In his own way, 007 mobilizes dissonant and dissident voices in relation to the dominant British culture: circulating languages and discourses, the spy brings out minority spaces of expression, making visible the edges and archipelagos in another relation to the world-culture.

Because he is open to the most diverse languages, James Bond creates a postcolonial counter-modernity, deploys a cultural hybridity and reinvents the linguistic and social imaginary. After a successful mission in Rome, the spy returns home to London in the opening scene of *Live and Let Die*. 007 is in the company of Miss Caruso, the Italian spy with whom he has completed his investigation. While M and his Italian counterpart search in vain for the spy, Bond and Caruso are together in London, talking in Italian: "Siamo sole," Bond tells her. "Alla fine", replies Caruso.

In *The Spy Who Loved Me*, James Bond joins his old Cambridge classmate, Sheik Hosein, who lives in a camp in the middle of the Egyptian desert. Dressed in traditional Bedouin garb, James Bond embarks on a long, silent journey across the desert on the back of his camel. Like a *fellahin*, he masters perfectly the driving of his animal, and knows the techniques of survival and orientation, in the middle of the dunes as far as the eye can see, in order not to get lost and to be able to find his way. 007 exchanges in Arabic with his guide: "Fatal qadir", he says to him, meaning that only a hero is able to make this way without getting lost. The two men arrive finally at a camp of nomads, near an oasis. "Shukraan," Bond said, easily seating his camel. As he enters the large Bedouin tent, he greets his friend who receives him: "As salma Alaykom," says 007, who adds in the direction of

Sheikh Hosein: "May Allah bless your home and welcome a poor itinerant."

Bond is as comfortable in the Egyptian desert on a camel as he is in the mountains of Afghanistan on a horse, fighting alongside the Mujahid Kamran Shah, former Oxford student and second-in-command of the Afghan district. 007 then takes part in an expedition with the Snow Cheetahs, mountain traffickers.

In *Nothing But Your Eyes*, when confronted with Melina Havelock, who is determined to avenge the death of her murdered marine archaeologists parents, Timothy and Iona Havelock, James Bond prefers to warn her. To this end, he quotes from memory a Chinese proverb from the fifth century B.C., taken from *Mencius*, the book of the philosopher Confucius: "He who seeks revenge should begin by digging two graves."

In *Tomorrow Never Dies*, 007 goes to Hamburg. He investigates the use of *fake news* by the multimedia destabilization group CMGN, the Carver communications. Bond perfectly masters the German language, he quickly deciphers the front page of the daily press, *Hamburger Abenblatt*, *Die Welt* or *Die Telegraf*, noticing in passing, like the spectator, that all the headlines of the German newsstand are identical, announcing then the standardization of the information.

Summing up 007's adaptability to every culture, Miss Moneypenny addresses James Bond in *Tomorrow Never Dies*: "You've always been a skilled linguist."

Through the use of cultural hybridity, which disrupts the notion of unique and exclusive belonging, Bond opens an enunciative space of dislocation and interstices. He implements a psychoanalytical reflection on national symptoms. Bond reinvents cinema as an interstitial and disjunctive space, a place where identities are blurred.

From this logic of discomfort and instability results a new cinematographic cartography. By multiplying shifts and blurs, Bond both modifies the thinking of cultural identities, by a plural poetics, and upsets the notion of subject, one and unique, by an aesthetics of wandering, where every being in the world is neither rooted nor sedentary, but is located outside of any fence.

Inscribed in a continuous flow of singularization and desubjectification, James Bond is a figure of the unpredictable, the unexpected and the friction.

As an explorer of languages and cultures, the secret agent 007 illustrates the image of the indivisible rhizome. As the philosopher and poet Édouard Glissant says: "Diversity is the matrix-motor of the chaos-world." We can say then that the diversity of cultures, present in the saga, announces the movement of a chaos-cinema: the unexpected gives rhythm to the action, gives a cadence to the image and a vivacity of pace to the screen. The James Bond films are part of a variation of identity, weaving the different into the exchange and the relationship. It is a cinema of energy and rupture, rather than a cinema of repetition. Against the same and the identical, Bond constantly reinvents himself and, as a result, also reinvents the cinema, which has become, thanks to him, a polyphony and a visual plasticity.

"My name is Bondov, Jerzy Bondov."

The British identity is gradually cracked, which underlines the adaptability of the character. In *The World Is Not Enough*, James Bond himself assumes this form of multicultural dissonance when he decides to call himself "Doctor Arkov, Mikhail Arkov", from the Russian Ministry of Atomic Energy. In another case, in *Killing is not Playing*, the change of nationality is done at his expense. Indeed, when James Bond is drugged and transported in an ambulance, General Georgi Koskov makes a false identity card for 007. It bears the name of "Jerzy Bondov", in order to easily pass the control services and to take James Bond by plane to an air base in Afghanistan.

The change of identity is already present by the diversity of nationality of some of its interpreters on screen. Depending on their place of birth, James Bond is in turn Scottish (Sean Connery was born in Edinburgh in 1930), Australian (George Lazenby is from Goulburn, where he was born in 1939), Welsh (Timothy Dalton was born in Colwyn Bay in 1946) or Irish (Pierce Brosnan was born in Drogheda in 1953). Even the actor of a parody trilogy, Mike Myers, is Canadian.

Globality is at the heart of the James Bond saga.

In fact, among the various inspirations, the real spy who served as a model for Ian Fleming to build his character is not an English agent, but a Serbian spy: the elegant and enigmatic Duško Popov.

Born in 1912 in the province of Vojvodina, in a milieu close to the Serbian royal family, Popov is a brilliant civil lawyer. Phlegmatic and seductive, a lover of alcohol and casinos, luxury hotels and sports cars, Popov is a Yugoslav secret agent. His code name is "Tricycle".

During World War II, Serbian spy Popov is a double agent: he works for the British, posing as a German ally. Popov was recruited by the secret organization, the Double Cross System, a British counter-intelligence committee supervised by John Cecil Masterman and headed by Thomas Argyll Robertson. This secret organization coordinates double agents in charge of infiltrating and deceiving the enemy. Duško Popov, out of anti-fascist conviction and British friendship, delivered false information to his German contact, a non-commissioned officer named Johann Jebsen. Towards the end of the war, Popov even managed to turn this German intelligence agent against the Nazi camp and to the benefit of the Allies. In addition, for several years, Popov deceived Hitler's master spy, Admiral Wilhelm Canaris, head of the Abwehr, the German army's intelligence service. At the risk of his life, Popov launched disinformation campaigns with the German general staff. He even succeeded in deciphering a German technique, the "microdot" principle. Invented by the German military intelligence, this process allows a simple dot printed on a sheet of paper, the same size as a dot on the "i" and read with a microscope, to reveal precious information.

Ian Fleming met Duško Popov in 1941 in the casino of the Hotel Paliccio in Estoril, a seaside resort on the Portuguese coast, west of Lisbon. He was impressed by the Serbian spy's coolness and elegance. Fleming witnessed Popov's bluff when he won a game of baccarat in the casino against a rich Lithuanian.

Elegant, casual and charming, a lover of champagne, a card and pool player, an accomplished sportsman and marksman, and a driver of big cars, Popov is a high-flying spy who plays a risky game. The German NCO, Von Karstoff, in charge of supervising Popov, had Popov pass loyalty tests, but the Serbian was doubling up the Abwehr for MI5.

While the British Intelligence Service greatly appreciated Popov's work, as Sir William Stephenson, nicknamed "Intrepid", the head of the British secret service during World War II, pointed out, the United States was mistrustful of him, wrongly so. The head of the FBI even refused to receive Popov who, alerted by essential information, made the trip to New York City.

Yet Popov is as knowledgeable as he is effective.

On the one hand, he gave false information to the Germans: through operation "Fortitude", he made the Reich troops believe that the Allied landings would not take place in Normandy, but much further north, on the Belgian coast.

On the other hand, Popov wanted to warn the head of the FBI, John Edgar Hoover, in person about the imminent

Japanese attack on Pearl Harbour. As the German Von Karstoff asked Popov for information about the state of the American submarines, the exact positions of the US ships, the location of the oil reserves, and the exact location of the hangars, Popov deduced that something was going on. Moreover, the Serbian spy understood, before anyone else, that the battle of Taranto, from November 11 to 12, 1940, when the Royal Navy bombed the Italian naval fleet, was going to inspire the same idea to the Japanese for their attack of December 7, 1941.

In vain: Hoover did not believe Popov. The bombing of the American port of Hawaii did take place, killing more than 2,400 Americans and wounding more than 1,200. Nobody moved before, despite Popov's warnings. Popov remained in New York City until October 1942. He then returned to Europe, managed to regain the trust of the Germans, and continued to spy on them.

A kaleidoscopic figure and a polysemous character, the spy Popov blurs the tracks of his own identity. Similarly, Agent 007 is not an authentic British subject. At least he embodies a multiple subject.

Aesthetic power of excess

In its own way, the James Bond saga reinvents the action and adventure film: fulgurating, powerful scenes, sonic and visual chaos, surging. The 007 films embody the great epic cinema.

While the material is based on triviality and reality (cars, guns, noises, explosions, destruction or demolitions), everything that in sum composes the classic imagery of combat, the artistic on screen consists in stylizing the whole to produce a transmutation of the images.

Action movies could be content with reproducing the noise of the world, or embodying the turmoil of reality: violence, conflicts, murders. With Bond, the chaos of cinema goes further. It reinvents new exchanges, new forms of identity. From violence, cinema gives rise to thought, an image-action in motion.

Thus a significant scene, extracted from *Licence to kill*. Thanks to a jerky rhythm of short shots, alternating close-up and general views, the dynamic editing of accelerated, superimposed and chained images intensifies space and time.

On the Paso del diablo road in Isthmus City, James Bond drives a tanker truck, chasing another vehicle. The maneuvering of the *truck*, sometimes on two rear wheels and sometimes on two side wheels, embodies an explosive, mechanical and visual rodeo. The alternation of the shots organizes a real chaos-cinema: four Kenworth W900B semi-trailers carrying their cargo of cocaine, six cars, a plane and four Stinger missiles. Between the aesthetics of the whirlwind and the choreography of the fair, the world is on the verge of explosion, filled with firecrackers and detonations. In a visual and sonic overkill, Bond uses his vehicle's *cruise control to* activate the vehicle's automatic pilot. The cinematic chaos then becomes a baroque, multicolored, overflowing spectacle: the trailers are projectiles that burst into flames and burn. No longer needing to drive his vehicle on the winding and tortuous roads of the labyrinthine asphalt, Bond climbs onto the roof of the tanker. He jumps onto the trailer in front of him. With the gasoline reserves threatening to explode at any moment, the final confrontation between James Bond and Franz Sanchez, the man with the iguana, takes place in an atmosphere of apocalypse, violence and frenzy.

But chaos-cinema is not limited, in the artistic work of the James Bond saga, to the sole dimension of violence and explosion. This chaos-cinema is also a spectacle that has its own theatricality. It reinvents the dramatic scene, where artifice and imagination are constantly turned upside down. Playing with the plunge and the counter-plunge, like chiaroscuro effects, between grandeur and decay, power and abandonment, light and darkness.

Chaos-cinema is a weaving of images and scenes where rhythms and tempos intermingle in a rhizomatic proliferation and a polyphonic fulgurance. This aesthetic of variation gives the film a vibrant epic breath. A mixture of visual syntaxes that confronts beings, bodies and things, in a sensational rhythmic ballet. A form of expressiveness, like a molten magma, of which James Bond is both the archaeologist and the director. What score does he play, when he is at the controls of an incredible tank, in the middle of the street of Saint Petersburg, in *GoldenEye*, or when he transforms his gondola into a hovercraft and thus crosses Saint Mark's Square in Venice, in *Moonraker*?

The sudden and unexpected explosion of the narrative framework leads to an aesthetic of chaos-cinema. A striking sequence of images, open to madness, dissonance and unleashed swells. Like an improvised freedom where, James Bond, maneuvering the most extraordinary toys, bursts the normative and the standardized to create a rocky, bubbling and cosmetic world.

When, in the aforementioned *GoldenEye*, James Bond drives a T-80 BV tank in the open air to rescue Natalya Simonova from the clutches of General Ourumov, who has been kidnapped in a car, 007 transforms the historic city of St. Petersburg. He drives into narrow streets, demolishes whole walls, crushes military jeeps and police cars. The 1,250 HP vehicle slides down the city boulevards as if on an ice rink. The tank skids in the middle of the street, destroys buildings, tears up roads, and crosses along the quays without stopping for a moment. The tank was so frightening to General Ourumov that he took out a flask of alcohol and nervously swallowed it as he watched his pursuer. The trucks and cars are no match for him. And the contrast is striking with the pilot of the tank, James Bond, who keeps his sense of humor and again shows a certain casualness, refusing to stick to his own identity. How to react to the aesthetics of agitation and to the process of total demolition? The casualness operates a distance to oneself and leads to a questioning of the fixed individuality. James' attitude is empirical: he acts in reaction to events and adapts to circumstances, in front of the raw, discontinuous and heterogeneous explosion of the world.

The city is on fire and blood, the streets are upside down. In the middle of a traffic circle, the tank crosses the entire urban space, without return or detour. Is it a game, a simple amusement? Suddenly, rushing towards the town hall, the float driven by Bond tore down the statue of a horseman placed in front of the town hall, and then continued its crazy race. This symbolic statue of Tsar Nicholas of Russia riding a winged horse remains on the float for a good part of the race. But just as the viewer hopes to catch his breath and get a break, Bond's tank ends up on a railroad track, facing an armored bunker train. "Full throttle, hit it!" the dreaded Janus orders the driver of the missile train, forced to comply.

Yes, *The World Is Not Enough*, the title of the nineteenth film in the saga, characterizes the universe of the Bond saga: a moving, teeming and vibrant filmic energy, constantly renewed, at the limit never reached, always further away, leading even beyond the boundaries of realism. A bubbling profusion, like a volcano, where the magma is born, gushes out and invades the screen.

Through its rhythms, leitmotifs and reiterations, chaos-cinema modifies and upsets the gaze through fluidity, intensity and simultaneity. The James Bond saga invents the chaos-cinema, that is to say the cinema of the passage, the interval and the metamorphosis. Never stable, never settled, it sets reality in motion and upsets the geopolitical scene. A flash or a breath, impossible to stop and to arrest.

For the philosopher Jean-Paul Sartre, cinema is the poem of modern life. It excels in the chiaroscuro, the mysterious mobility, the fantastic acceleration. In other words the aesthetics of the contingency. Such is the sign of the chaos-cinema in the heart of the saga 007: in a conference given in front of his students in the high school of Le Havre, Sartre describes "these interlaces where events full of sense are inserted, [...] this scattering of actions which makes place, all of a sudden, to dazzling unions and soon broken."

Chaos-cinema combines two dimensions, that of the virtuoso visual technique and that of the unclassifiable baroque-world.

The technical power is breathtaking: the intense camera movement, the oversized means are at the service of a hallucinatory spectacle. With cult and impressive scenes, both in terms of editing and direction: the explosive final rodeo in *Licence to Kill*, the tank in the middle of the street of St Petersburg in *GoldenEye*, the bulldozer on a construction site in Madagascar in *Casino Royale* or the backhoe used by Bond to connect the parts of the train, at the opening of *Skyfall*. So many technical aspects and visual overkill that only Bond films can offer. Thanks to studios, specialized teams and unique means. A director who is not used to this blockbuster cinema has experienced this: during his inaugural lecture in October 2018 at the Collège de France, where he is the first filmmaker appointed to the annual chair of Artistic Creation, director Amos Gitai refers to Pinewood Studios, near London, "where all James Bond films are made."

It was there, he explains, that he got in touch with an incredible English team, able to install a hydraulic system to shoot the scene of one of his films and to solve the difficulty of suspending a Bell 205 helicopter, the camera and the actors inside, the landscape in the background. "You have to work out a logistical strategy to serve the ideas of the mise en scène," says the author of *Kadosh* and *Kippur*. Because how to film? In what visual language and with what cinematographic syntax? Between the noise of the helicopter and that of the explosions, between the physical movement of the bodies and the agitation of the displacements, to direct means to create a structure in the agitation, thanks to the chaos-cinema. "Shooting a film requires a certain tenacity," concludes Amos Gitai, recalling his preparatory work with the stagehands at Pinewood Studios. Filming implies a physical and moral commitment, not only aesthetic or artistic. At the heart of the mythical Pinewood Studios is the 007 Stage, one of the largest film sets in the world. This magical and unusual place was originally built by the set designer Ken Adam to build the interior of the *supertanker* of *The Spy Who Loved Me*.

With the James Bond cinema, we are embarked in an indivisible and jostling current, powerful and uninterrupted: a work made of brief and elusive reminders, of deep and secret sensations. Such is the universe of 007. A world based on simulacra and pretense, then transcended thanks to a surfeit of special effects and grand spectacle explosions.

But there is a second dimension to this chaos-cinema: a baroque theater, worthy of the *Comedia dell'arte*, where simulacra and magic occupy all the space. James Bond is a character of illusion and prestidigitation, a figure suspended in the air who flies like a marvelous puppet. No doubt it is this dimension of Neapolitan theater and baroque composition in him that so seduced Federico Fellini.

One day, the author of *La Strada*, *Amarcord* and *And the Ship Went Away* wrote to his producer, Dino de Laurentiis, and told him that he wanted to make a "metaphysical James Bond". The film, as Fellini imagines it, will be grandiose and disproportionate, a blockbuster including thousands of costumes, created by Pier Luigi Pizzi, or the construction of a train with eight floors. Who will play the hero 007? Fellini is already thinking of Gregory Peck, Steve McQueen or Paul Newman. The actors came especially to Rome to discuss the role with the master. But the film will not be made.

However, the idea is there: the chaos-cinema is an aesthetic laboratory of contingency and power, of life and death, of excess and violence.

Beyond Britishness and globality. It is clear that, in this universe, James Bond can no longer be defined simply by the permanence of his being (a British subject), but that, carried along by the multidirectional action and the permeability of his shifting identities, he adapts to the vagaries of the world, a hybrid, multiple and cosmopolitan figure. Such is the second secret of 007.

3. FROM DANDYISM TO ROMANTICISM, THE COMEDY OF *OVERMARRIAGE*

"Madeleine Swann:
*Why, among so many possibilities,
choose a life as a hitman?*
James Bond:
It was either that or a priest."
Spectrum

A figure of masculinity and virility, James Bond symbolizes irresistible seduction, in the classic tradition of *serial lovers*. But is the eroticism of the series purely conventional, in a unilateral relationship with women, or does it operate a critical distance that disturbs the classic paradigm of male power? Can a philosophical reading complexify the erotic and loving relationships of the secret agent? Thus, among the possible interpretations, when 007 comes out of the turquoise waters of the Bahamas, wearing a sky-blue *shorty* swimsuit, in *Casino Royale*, the multiple representation of masculinity can make him, as a sexualized and eroticized body, a gay and queer icon. Would 007 then embody a sexual fantasy, as much homosexual as heterosexual? Deciphering the bisexuality of the British hero and his attraction to men and women on screen is part of the renewal of the plural LGBTQIA+ movements - lesbian, gay, bi, trans, queer, intersex and their allies. Indeed, the physical plastic of James Bond does not leave insensitive several men, as Le Chiffre or Silva. The latter, under the spell of the agent during a sensual scene of seduction in *Skyfall*, caresses the torso of 007 who answers: "What makes you think it's my first time?" Far from an exclusive male domination and mysoginy of another time, James Bond is a man with assumed fragility, able to embody a body alternately vulnerable and desiring, submissive and dominant. Moreover, beyond their professional complicity, is there not a reciprocal attraction in the faithful relationship between James Bond and Felix Leiter? And if everything is replayed in male relationships, what about female desires and games of seduction? Thus, with James Bond, the relations of the masculine and the feminine are redistributed. The 007 saga blurs classical conventions and traditional paradigms.

The spy dresses in Prada

If you open Baudelaire's little essay *The Painter of Modern Life*, published in three issues in November and December 1863 in *Le Figaro*, you will discover the titles of the different chapters: "Beauty, Fashion and Happiness", "The Artist, Man of the World [...]", "Modernity", "The Annals of War", "The Military", "The Dandy", "In Praise of Make-up", "Women and Girls" and "Cars". These themes, which announce each part of Baudelaire's text, immediately evoke the figure of James Bond and his aesthetic universe. It is as if the poet were delivering to us, through his prophetic intuition, the power of the myth of James Bond, "hero of modern life", a hundred years before the first film of the saga. There was the portrait of the dandy-poet; there is now that of the dandy-spy.

Do his elegance and distinction make 007 a perfect dandy, a refined gentleman? What does the *James Bond way of life* tell us about his way of being and his art of dressing? A secret agent who loves the best champagnes, Taittinger, Dom Pérignon or Bollinger, can only emphasize his attraction for the brightness of life and claim the sparkle of existence. Nothing is too good for Her Majesty's special spy: when, in *Quantum of Solace*, the liaison agent Miss Fields takes James Bond to a second-rate hotel, located in a turbulent district of La Paz and reserved for him by the British consulate, 007 refuses to stay there. However their cover obliges them to discretion and to an alibi: "We must have the air of professors in availability", insists the agent Fields. "Rather sleep in the morgue", adds 007 who prefers to leave the place immediately and to stay in a five stars luxury hotel. He takes Fields with him and tells the maitre d' who welcomes them in a luxurious setting: "We're teachers on vacation, but we won the lottery," says Bond, determined to take advantage of the hotel's most beautiful suite.

Bond's luxurious taste for appearances, sometimes light or futile, also manifests itself in his clothing choices, as a desire to assert his individualism. From the blue polo shirt and pants in *James Bond vs. Doctor No* in 1962, to the grey Brioni suit in *The World is Not Enough* in 1999, to the dark three-piece suit at the end of *Casino Royale* in 2006, Agent 007 is a *fashion victim*. He carefully chooses the most diverse appearances that reflect his being-in-the-world and embody his mode of action and the distinction of his commitment. For Bond, a tuxedo is a combat armor, but also an unusual garment: the outfit he wears signals the will to mark his difference and to cultivate his singularity, in a normalized and standardized world.

Buoyed by the artefact and trompe-l'oeil of his sophisticated gadgets and miniature weapons, Bond develops a stylistic strategy at the heart of his attitude and behaviour. He is a man who loves speed and acceleration, who seeks risk and danger. Intoxicated by driving spectacular cars - invisible, amphibious, aerial and sophisticated - 007 pilots these vehicles with style. At the wheel of a mythical Aston Martin DB5, with hydraulic bumper and radar screen, or a Lotus Esprit that can be transformed into a submarine, Bond embodies the art of living of the *goldenboy* or the *playboy*. The speed of off-road and off-road driving is found in every machine driven by the hero: bobsled, switchblade or hovercraft. Moreover, the recurrent way in which he presents his passion for frequenting gambling tables and casinos also signals another characteristic trait of his personality. If 007 is addicted to men's fashion, his passion for card games shows both his determination to win and his taste for risk. What Baudelaire calls "the last burst of heroism in decadence".

In fact, the cinematographic setting is not mistaken: the very first appearance of James Bond in the saga takes place in a gaming room, "The Ambassadors' Circle", in London. During the card game called "The Railway Game", we do not see his face, but only his hands that manipulate and throw the cards. The seductive effect is immediate, not only on Sylvia Trench, his partner in the game, but also on the spectator. Then, it is through Trench's eyes that we suddenly see Bond's hands. They reach into his case and pull out a cigarette, which he lights with his lighter. The flame lights up his face as he utters the most famous line in film history: "My name is Bond, James Bond.

In a few moments, from a glance at the hands to an attentive listening of the voice, a style and an attitude are established.

Bond not only has an addictive taste for elegant dress, but also the pleasure of challenging his opponents around the gaming table. Sometimes his passion for cards leads him to take crazy risks. During a card game in the private room of a hotel casino in Montenegro, a game of *no-limit hold'em* poker whose rules have been reminded to the various players by the Swiss banker from Basel, Mendel, in *Casino Royale*, Bond has to deal with a formidable opponent, a ventolin assassin, Le Chiffre. In the first one-on-one game, Le Chiffre wins, making Bond think he was bluffing: he wins by a square of jacks. After an eventful episode, Bond returns to the table. This time, the stakes are raised and he is in the $15 million pot. After a risky game, Bond wins *in extremis* with a straight flush. He has the best hand, 8, 7, 6, 5 and 4 in spades. One of the most famous games of golf in cinema takes place on the greens of Stoke Park, a famous English country club owned by Bond's sporting opponent, Auric Goldfinger. The latter, ready to do anything to win the game and the coveted Nazi gold bullion, uses another Slazenger 1 ball, cheated by his caddy and henchman, Oddjob, when the first ball is lost somewhere on the course. Bond, who has figured out the deception, lets Goldfinger play, but substitutes a Slazenger 7 for the Slazenger 1 during the game, without the businessman noticing. On the last hole, Bond points out that it's the wrong ball, and Goldfinger loses the point and the match. Casual, clever and cunning, 007 knows that confrontation with an enemy often takes place during a game or a match, in the casino or on a golf green.

Alongside 007's almost aristocratic characteristics, such as his enjoyment of the game and elegant dress, Bond's tumultuous relationship with his superiors at MI6, especially his chief M, a figure of order and law, is also a feature of dandyism.

The spy often goes beyond the order he has received. The hero does as he pleases and prefers to take dangerous, uncontrollable or risky initiatives rather than respecting the classic protocol and the usual procedure. Why does this happen? How does Bond justify his deviations from proper conduct? His disobedience is guided by instinct and initiative: in his own special way, Bond still wants to carry out his missions, but in the way he alone has decided to go. With his hands tied, M is accountable for his agent: above the head of MI6 in the hierarchy of administrative authority are the Foreign Secretary, the Home Secretary and the Chairman of the Intelligence and Security Committee. They too are subject to the will and decision of the British Prime Minister. In the world of secret political organizations, each security service is dependent on another. Anyone who works in the bureaucracy must submit to the strict administrative hierarchy.

But on several occasions, 007's attitude is on the verge of creating a diplomatic incident within the British house. If they show an effective originality and an acute sense of anticipation, the slips of Bond pass, in the eyes of his superiors, for negligence or incompetence.

In *Operation Thunderbolt*, the Minister of the Interior asks M: "Does your agent 007 have a lead?" M replies, "False alarm unfortunately," and the minister, annoyed, adds, "Your agent seems to have a knack for suspense." This shows that, with 007, the narrative *drama* is on the razor's edge, and can swing one way or the other at any moment. The outcome is uncertain, as Bond is perceived as unstable. In *Quantum of Solace,* M is summoned to the Foreign Secretary's office, who criticizes the head of MI6 for letting the spy run wild: "In foreign policy, no hunch or hint." During this large-scale mission against a terrorist organization, whose objective is to help dictators succeed in their coup d'état in South America, with the complicity of the CIA, in order to seize for their own account areas of drinking water and thus control territories, M tries several times to block Bond. During a telephone connection between England and Austria, M insists to his agent: "Come to the report!" The secret agent replies, "No time." M is desperate to see Bond eliminate one by one all the people who could lead to the trail of the terrorist organization: the traitor and double agent Craig Mitchell shot by Bond in Siena, the assassin Edmund Slate killed by Bond at the Hotel Dessalines in Port-au-Prince, the bodyguard of Guy Haines, corrupt advisor to the British Prime Minister, dropped by Bond into the void from the top of the Bregenz opera house. M insists to his agent, "Control yourself and limit your fire. Get inside!" But Bond disobeys again, "I'd love to, but first I have to find whoever wanted to kill you." So M decides to cut his agent loose and asks his right-hand man, Bill Tanner, to immobilize Bond: cancel his credit cards and block his passports. M, accompanied by MI6 agents, is even obliged to follow Bond to the Grand Hotel Andrean, in La Paz, Bolivia, to try to stop him. But, once in the elevator and handcuffed, Bond, suspended from his functions and having given his weapon of service, gets rid nevertheless of his guards of the MI6 and runs away in English. "Go home!" suggests M to Bond again, in the film's final scene set in Kazan, the capital of Tatarstan seven hundred kilometers east of Moscow, but Bond tells him, "I never left."

In the end, in the eyes of his superiors, Bond is still the best MI6 agent, as shown in the last scene of *Nothing But Your Eyes*, when the Prime Minister himself wants to thank him. Flattered by such an honor for their agent, Q and the Minister of Defense manage to obtain a satellite link between *10 Downing Street* in the British capital and the *Triana* in the Aegean Sea, the ship of Melina Havelock's parents where Bond is staying. Unconcerned with protocol as much as reward, and wishing to enjoy the midnight swim, Bond lets Margaret Thatcher converse with Max, the Havelocks' faithful parrot.

A dialectical tension between love and hate runs through all the relationships between James Bond and his superiors. 007's bosses rely on him, aware of his real and effective skills, but disapprove of his improvised and solitary methods. Bond is a hothead. The paradoxes of disobedience and persistence, refusal and obstinacy, loyalty and infidelity, are at the heart of 007's dandyism. Baudelaire, once again, gives a precise explanation: "Dandyism plays with the rule and yet still respects it. He suffers from it and takes revenge on it while undergoing it; he claims it when he escapes from it; he dominates it and is dominated by it in turn." For his part, the writer Jules Barbey d'Aurevilly, in his treatise *Du dandysme*, also evokes the attitude of protest peculiar to the rebel dandy: "It is an individual revolution against the established order."

Tensions are frequent between M and Bond: exchange and communication between them is difficult. But beyond the dandyism, Bond faces a crucial ethical issue: is he acting personally or professionally? Should he do his duty or seek revenge? James Bond is a hero with many flaws, who can be driven by the anger of a vendetta and the spirit of revenge. The sign of retaliation is symbolized by the lighter in *Licence to Kill*, given to Bond by his two friends at the time of their wedding and on which we can read: "James. Love Always, Della and Felix." And when Della and Felix Leiter are kidnapped by Franz Sanchez, whose law is *Plomo o plata* ("Lead or money"), Bond vows to avenge them. Della is murdered, Felix violently tortured and mutilated. During his dangerous mission in Isthmus City, 007 uses the lighter, a gift from the newlyweds, as the ultimate weapon to get rid of the drug dealer.

007 is an elusive individual. It is difficult to unravel his mysteries because Bond seems sometimes blinded by vengeful grief, sometimes motivated by moral rectitude. The question then arises: when a mission is too close to his heart, should he go through with it? Should he stop or continue, but at what cost? Bond acts according to his feelings and his sensitivity. Yet he knows this better than anyone when, his emotions somewhat calmed, he confesses to M: "The dead don't care about being avenged."

By revenge or by taste for risk, by obstinacy or by loyalty, 007 wants to put his mark and his style on each of his missions, at the risk of disobeying and compromising his hierarchy. In doing so, acting according to a personal imperative above norms and conformities, Bond embodies the true dandy: a man, alone, in the middle of the crowd.

His personal taste for luxury and action is also evident on numerous occasions, between golf tournaments, sports cars or luxury boats, custom-made suits and games of poker, bridge or baccarat. Sure of his charm and elegance, James Bond plays his seduction at every moment. And in each of his adventures, Agent 007 turns to women. James Bond enjoys female company, but to what end? What does this attraction mean to him?

The time of the lovers

Eroticism and sex are in the heart of the universe of 007, in the center of the relations that James maintains with his female partners. The secret agent claims the sexual freedom and defends a way of life tendentially libertine.

Multiplying the conquests and the amorous experiments, sometimes with his partners of mission, sometimes with his direct adversaries, Bond incarnates the free and individual spirit of the great libertine. The quest for carnal pleasure is accompanied by the rejection of the established dogmas and conventions in force. If 007 is the most nonconformist spy of MI6, sexuality takes part of his taste of the game and his rejection of the rules.

James Bond is a hedonist and a jouster in his own way. He takes advantage of pleasures. Gifted in the games of seduction and manipulation, Bond knows how to take advantage of situations and tries to make them evolve to his advantage. Engaging in subtle dialogue, touching the sensibilities of the person he meets or arousing his interest: Bond has learned his lesson from Machiavelli's *Prince*. 007 follows the recommendation made by Machiavelli, the Florentine pragmatic philosopher, to those who want to lead or govern: be as cunning as a fox or as ferocious as a lion. Strength and cunning involve disguising, deceiving and killing, but also seducing, manipulating and, in the manner of Bond, multiplying love affairs. In *Operation Thunder*, the secret agent enjoys a fitness break at the Shrublands clinic in Sussex. But he almost gets killed on a traction table set at full speed. The osteopath rushes to rescue him, then asks 007 to keep silent about this incident. The spy accepts, in exchange of a love session in the hot fumes of the *turkish bath of the* clinic.

If Bond refuses authority, he seeks pleasure, sometimes in a clandestine way because the taste of pleasure is always in the secret.

His libertine model is undoubtedly Giacomo Casanova, who, like 007, is at the same time an adventurer who loves danger, a spy by profession in the service of political diplomacy and a traveler around the world. In *The Story of My Life*, Casanova recounts his exploits in love and sexual practices with one hundred and forty-two women. Does the James Bond saga do anything else? In the films, 007 is a libertine in the sense that he wants to conquer, for the love of the game, and seduce, for the pleasure of the challenge. His light, playful and irresponsible morality is closer to the carnival of Casanova than to the cruelty of the Viscount Valmont, the violence of Sade or the desire of Don Juan. Bond is a naval *commander*, as Choderlos de Laclos, the libertine author of *Dangerous Liaisons*, was an artillery officer: the seduction of a woman as a conquest to be led, a battle plan to be established and a siege strategy to be consolidated. Yes, love in 007 is first of all a mental and psychic game, a psychological game of gallantry, courtesy and flirting. The erotic stake is there: to walk through the world and to take advantage of the women, to enjoy the meetings made according to the missions.

If James Bond is first seen as the ideal of the dandy, he is also the archetype of the libertine. His main concern is immediate, impulsive and impulsive happiness, provided by pleasure and sensations. Bond is a gourmet, crazy about wine and alcohol, obsessed with the suits and fabrics he wears. If the spy is sometimes taciturn and melancholic, the company of women suddenly makes him amiable, cheerful, passionate about conversations and carried away by the most diverse subjects. His spirit of adventure, pleasure and curiosity is his only true guide.

Again, like Casanova, Bond is a solitary nomad who shuns boring company as he stubbornly seeks the charms of pleasure. Bond travels the world; Casanova stays from Rome to Constantinople, from London to Moscow or Trieste. Bond travels for sixty-eight years through twenty-five films, between 1962 and 2020; Casanova also travels the world for sixty-three years, from 1734 to 1797. For both adventurers and spies, movement is vital, the energy is in the movement, the momentum is permanent. To satisfy their desires, to discover the world, to escape and fly away, to follow their only pleasures, or almost, because the missions are there and the dangers too. But the pleasure lasts. Besides, Bond and Casanova both speak French easily, and French is the language of love.

Is there a London libertinism, as there is a Venetian libertinism? In fact, the city of Casanova is a destination regularly chosen by 007, which reinforces his attraction for libertinage. Venice is the city of pleasure: Bond goes there several times, mixing sex and investigation. In the City of the Doges, or Serenissima, 007 is always in good company: with Tatiana Romanova in *Goodbye Russia*, with Holly Goodhead in *Moonraker*, with Vesper Lynd in *Casino Royale*.

With James Bond sex can also be cruel. The passion of bodies often announces death. As Miranda Frost, MI6 agent, fencing champion and secret mistress of Colonel Moon, tells 007: "M warned me about you. You offer sex as an appetizer, death as a dessert, no thanks." In the adventures of 007, the spy's wives and lovers sometimes meet a disastrous fate.

Violence and eroticism are mixed, sensuality and perversity meet. *James Bond ladies* are murdered, in reprisal for their choice of love and for having given in to the hero's advances. The other side of the coin to the love game is the taste of danger, or death that strikes. "Dying" is announced in the title of many films, *Living and Letting Die*, *Tomorrow Never Dies*, *Die Another Day* or *Dying Can Wait*.

Golden or dark, sparkling or black, gold kills. Twice. In *Goldfinger*, James Bond gets close to Jill Masterson, who helps him get Auric Goldfinger to lose at cards to Simmons by the pool of the Fontainebleau Hotel in Miami. To punish her for her betrayal, Jill Masterson's naked body is covered with a thin gold paint or film from head to toe. When Bond discovers Jill's body, asphyxiated or mummified by the gold, he barely dares to touch her and simply brushes against her, flying over her neck.

In *Quantum of Solace*, the lifeless body of Agent Fields is discovered coated in crude oil in Bond's hotel room. His death is not in retaliation for a betrayal because Fields works for the British consulate in Bolivia. But his murderer, Dominic Greene, chooses to eliminate him with black gold to put the British and American governments on the wrong track, the search by the terrorist organization of a supposed oil reserve in the Bolivian desert.

If not by yellow gold or black gold, death strikes at every moment those who give themselves to 007, from the helicopter pilot Corinne Dufour in *Moonraker* to Paris Carver in *Tomorrow Never Dies* or Séverine in *Skyfall*.

After having helped 007 and spent the night with him in his room, in the sumptuous castle of the Mojave desert, Corinne Dufour dies the next day in the forest of the property, hunting game devoured by the dogs of Hugo Drax. In this hyper-realistic scene, where the dramatic tension is carried by the movement of the camera, right in the bushes of the forest, the young woman is pursued and killed by the three ferocious Dobermans.

In the guise of a banker, James Bond goes to Hamburg and attends the launch party of the global telecommunications satellite network of tycoon Elliot Carver, a specialist in disinformation and *fake news*. There he meets up with a former mistress, Paris Carver, who has become the wife of the CEO of *Tomorrow's news*, a digital network empire worthy of the GAFAs and capable of destabilizing the media. After having slapped 007, Paris Carver says to him with derision: "You always sleep with a gun under your pillow? You want to make me talk with charm. " But still in love with 007, she ends up giving in to his advances. Later, Bond discovers her lifeless body in her hotel room, while at the same time, the television station is already announcing the death of the wife of the president of the news channel. Paris Carver is murdered by Dr. Kaufman, a specialist in criminal medicine and her husband's personal killer.

Former prostitute of Macao, Séverine meets 007 in the casino of the Floating Dragon. She proposes to him to join her at night on the yacht *La Chimère*. The two lovers share an intimacy in the shower of the boat. On waking up, captured with Bond by Tiago Rodriguez on his desert island, Séverine is killed in cold blood with a pistol by Silva, who puts on her head a glass of Macallan 1962 whisky before shooting.

But the women in the adventures of the saga are not only tragic victims of the bloodthirsty violence and murderous madness of men. They are neither reduced to sacrificial beings, nor limited to sexual desires. The female characters are heroines and alter egos, equal to the British agent, regularly saving his ass. Far from the ridiculous stereotype of the pin-up girl or the vulgar cliché of the playmate, a concern for gender equality runs through the saga. Not always, it is true, as a reality already effective on the screen, but more as a project in the making or a cinematographic ideal to conquer. Nevertheless, the women of action, adventurers and committed, are very present. They accompany the secret agent in his quest and accomplish the mission with the same success as their male counterpart.

A member of NASA's research administration, Holly Goodhead is not only an astrophysicist and space engineering specialist, but also an elite CIA spy and fighter. Her skills as a cosmonaut and rocket pilot are essential in orbit, in the Space City, to stop Drax's evil plan to destroy humanity from his laboratory experiments on the plant *Orchidae nigra*.

Armed with her crossbow, Melina Havelock takes justice into her own hands and kills Hector Gonzales with an arrow: "I'm half Greek," she explains to 007, "and Greek women, like Electra, always avenge their loved ones." At a depth of one hundred and seventy-eight meters, she and Bond pilot the two-seater submarine *Neptune*, in order to recover the ATAC transmitter system from the wreck of the ship *Saint-Georges-Valletta with the* help of divers. With Milos Colombo, James Bond and a few others, Melina Havelock participates in the perilous ascent of Mount St. Cyril. With the help of winch, pulley and basket, they climb the mountain to the hideout of Aris Kristatos, who is hiding, planning to escape to Cuba, in an old abandoned orthodox monastery.

Many of 007's allies and lovers are high-tech spies, with a cold-bloodedness and efficiency that knows no bounds. Russian Commander Anya Amasova, a KGB Agent X, meets Bond at the site of the Giza Pyramids, near the tomb of Khufu, Pharaoh of the Fourth Dynasty. Together they meet Max Kalba at the Mujaba Club in Cairo and confront Jaws in an Egyptian open-air temple. General Alexis Gogol confirms to his MI6 counterpart M the necessity of associating Triple X and 007: "Two such perceptive brains will appreciate working together in the name of the new Anglo-Soviet cooperation."

The erotic-political association also works with Aki, the Japanese Secret Service (SIS) spy 294, who repeatedly saves Bond from the clutches of Osato's guards. On another mission, 007 is helped by Pam Bouvier, a freelance pilot and CIA agent. Alongside Bond, at the Barrelhead bar in Bimini, protected by a Kevlar bulletproof vest, Pam Bouvier bravely confronts Franz Sanchez's henchmen, especially the cruel Dario, with a high-caliber rifle. Such an association is repeated with Wai Lin, a colonel of the Chinese territorial defense services. Working for Chinese external security, Wai Lin is able to drive a motorcycle while handcuffed to Bond, and disable four cars and a helicopter that chase them, still attached to 007, through the streets and rooftops of Saigon. Then, alone, she confronts fifteen ninjas that she knocks out, without using her service weapon, a Makarov 59. Elsewhere, on another mission, Bond teams up with Jinx, an NSA agent, to prevent Gustav Graves from destroying South Korean defenses with the *Icarus* satellite. He is also seen teaming up with Dr. Christmas Jones, a nuclear physicist who works for the International Decommissioning Agency (IDA). Jones and Bond together discover the plan of the terrorist Renard and his accomplice Elektra King who want to destroy and contaminate with plutonium the Bosphorus Strait and the surroundings of Istanbul. In *Dying Can Wait*, Bond and Nomi, 007's new colleague at MI6, are both licensed to kill and both have secret agent licenses.

Without the determination and intervention of the female characters, James Bond would not have survived for long and would have died more than once. The games of action, love and chance are the three-dimensional key to 007's filmic adventures. The sensual cartography of the female characters determines the relationships between men and women in Bond films. In general, the spy flits and twirls according to his encounters: he is ready to seduce a florist in Cortina d'Ampezzo, to fall into the arms of an Italian aristocrat - Countess Lisl von Schlaf, with whom Bond poses as a writer preparing a novel about Greek smugglers - or to follow a virtuoso cellist to the ends of the earth, who never leaves her Stradivarius and who dreams of playing for him at Carnegie Hall in New York City.

With James Bond, the portrait of a charming dandy, a hedonistic libertine and a pleasure-seeking adventurer takes shape.

Seeking the favors of *James Bond women*, the seducer, who displays freedom as a principle of life, takes on the traits of the secret agent. His mode of existence corresponds to the description made by Baudelaire, in the final synthesis of the *Painter of the modern life*: neither sentimental, "the dandy does not aim at love", nor greedy, "the dandy does not aspire to the money", it is initially a singular individual. "It is above all the ardent need to make an originality" that characterizes him, says Baudelaire. This makes James Bond a spy apart, unique and out of the ordinary.

As for his character and personality, Baudelaire concludes, "a dandy can be a jaded man, can be a suffering man." This is indeed the case with 007: his psychology shows him sometimes disturbed and sometimes insensitive, either tormented by a personal suffering, or marked by a form of detachment, absence and distance. But, as Baudelaire says, the dandy has "this attitude of provocative caste, even in his coldness". It should be noted that this coldness, which in reality masks a deep distress, is well present in the interpretation of Bond, by the play of Daniel Craig in particular: his license allowing him, the secret agent is a cold-blooded killer. Baudelaire was right: "The beauty of the dandy consists above all in the cold air that comes from the unshakeable resolution not to be moved. Cold and unemotional, Bond is not completely so, but he is capable of being so when the situation demands it. In the opening scene of *Casino Royale*, filmed in black and white, amidst the mists, in a retro style to evoke a distant memory and a return to his roots, Bond gets his "00" number in Prague, Czech Republic. Bond's first two official targets are Fisher and Dryden, two MI6 traitors. He eliminates the former "painfully" and the latter "extremely", and in both cases demonstrates a calmness, control and aplomb that fully justifies his recent authorization to kill.

The best dandy there is, Baudelaire concludes, is neither French nor Italian, but English. Indeed, for the poet, the master of elegance and the arbiter of fashion can only be an Englishman. It is thus again of 007 of which it is a question, when Baudelaire writes: "The dandies make themselves more and more rare among us, while among our neighbors, in England, the social state and the Constitution will still leave a place for a long time to the heirs of Sheridan, Brummell and Byron, if however it presents some who are worthy of it." There is no doubt that 007 is "worthy". He asserts himself as a worthy heir of the most radical dandyism and the most profound libertinism.

On the level of desire, eroticism occupies the main part of male and female relationships, like Bond's wild, sensual and even violent sexuality with the evil Xenia Sergueievna Onatopp.

Cruel and killer, this Georgian is a former helicopter pilot of the USSR, suspected, from the beginning of *GoldenEye,* of links with the mafia of the "Janus" organization of Saint Petersburg. When they meet in Monte Carlo, Bond tells her, in sexual defiance: "We have the same passions, three at least." Then he clarifies: "I count two: car racing and baccarat." With Onatopp, sex no longer becomes a game of pleasure but a torture of the opponent, which Bond refuses during their erotic session in the sauna of a hotel in St. Petersburg.

If, in general, Bond gives in easily to his sexual impulses, does he seek only erotic pleasure in relationships with women? What does he really want? Who or what is Bond after? The quest for pure enjoyment, between refinement and hedonism, is perhaps only an appearance. What if Bond sublimates eroticism for something else? If we take a closer look, Agent 007 is in permanent search of what we will call in this chapter "overmarriage".

We have loved each other so much

If a secret agent is generally defined by his absence of interpersonal link, neither affect nor empathy, 007 is the exact opposite: romantic, vulnerable, sensitive, he gets personally involved in the couple and seeks to settle in a long term relationship. So one wonders: would the apparent seducer actually hide a genuine lover? Behind the hedonism can a neo-romantic and post-sentimental figure be hidden?

Through his erotic conquests, Bond would be in search of absolute union and ideal love. Love, the real one, the one you feel with only one woman, for whom you are madly in love. Instead of a saga based on the erotic games of marivaudage, the James Bond series would be first and foremost a comedy of "overmarriage", in the tradition of the American Hollywood romances of the 1930s. As we sometimes say "overwork", or talk about "overbilling", James Bond is regularly a candidate for "overmarriage". Each project of seduction or conquest is not a response to erotic desire alone, but the quest for a true union, made to last a lifetime, sought by the hero.

Miracle in London or English marriage? One could only wish him to live an eternal fairy tale, but fate has not quite decided so: the closer James Bond gets to happiness, the more he escapes it. He is actually attracted to marriage, which desperately refuses him. Regularly subjected to the loss of the beloved woman, real wife or on the point of being one, 007 is marked in his flesh, he is an individual in suffering. His love relationship is that of the diabolical lovers who cannot live happily and are destroyed, devastated. Through the adventures of 007, it is the quest for an impossible love.

The marriage is always presented here as an unattainable desire. This dream haunts every film and pursues every relationship that 007 has with a woman. We must then speak about "over-marriage": since it is impossible for him, marriage is transformed into obsession, haunting, desire, madness or fantasy. This over-investment is the explanatory key of the films of the saga. Because the spy thriller is not here a simple phenomenon of visual and spectacular action, or a series of incredible adventures and breathtaking scenes. No, the secret service film becomes a romantic melodrama.

This is his new secret: the goal sought by James Bond is not the marivaudage of bodies or the multi-sexual frolic, but the wish, the vow of monogamous nuptials. In truth, James Bond is obsessed with a sacred commitment, and, like all impossible ideals, marriage becomes, as the films progress, a mixture of fantasy and simulacrum. For the spy, who evolves in a world where danger and death are permanent, the idea of marriage can only be lived in the interstitial space of dreams. The "super-marriage", defined as utopia and pure image, is a fantasy overhanging the saga. The blessing of the union of the couple obsesses the hero.

In *James Bond versus Doctor No*, the appearance of Honey Rider, a shellfish fisherwoman whose biologist and oceanographer father was killed by Doctor No, immediately seduces 007 and triggers his matrimonial fantasy. But is the simulacrum of the Amazon or naiad emerging from the turquoise water on a Caribbean beach a dream or a reality? For the spectator also, the goddess of femininity or the aquatic nymph who takes the appearance of this swimmer-diver is a fantasy. Bond, for his part, attends the scene a little in the background. He can only dream of the apparition: he sublimates this epiphany, desires it and imagines it. Moreover, on the screen, the hero can only enter the scene to the tune of a song: hardly daring to interrupt the bather, 007 begins to sing *Under the Mango Tree*, which Honey Rider is humming as she emerges from the water. Yes, the meeting of the two lovers begins like a musical, a real Hollywood romance.

In the eyes of James Bond, fascinated by the spectacle of beauty, Honey Rider embodies a pure, almost unreal and unattainable image of femininity. Despite this impossible desire, one scene shows the loving complicity and sensitive bond between Bond and the woman he has just met on the forbidden beach, who is determined to take revenge on Doctor No. A philosophical reading of the scene detects a dreamed and imagined marriage: when Sister Rose and Sister Lilly invite the two prisoners to dress in appropriate Chinese attire for dinner, the heroine confides to the young man who accompanies her: "Your hands are sweaty. So are mine." Then Bond replies, "Yes, I'm scared too." This rapprochement announces the creation of the loving couple, based on complicity and reciprocity, capable of sharing common emotions and sensations. But isn't having sweaty hands together also an emotional and physical state that we feel when we come together at the altar to celebrate the union between two people who love each other? The wetness of the hands can be seen as a form of announcing the marriage, while the actual situation is very different. Regularly, in the saga, the end of the film takes the form of a honeymoon: Rider and Bond manage to escape in a small motorboat, before running out of fuel in the middle of the ocean and being towed away by the military shuttle of the United States Marine Police, on which Felix Leiter is sitting. The *happy ending*, "They got married, lived happily ever after and had many children", is only a supposed dream imagined by the viewer, once the screen is turned off. A fantasy of "over-marriage", again.

A romantic hero, whether willingly or unwillingly, Bond is not a mere runner. On the contrary, romance is a regular feature of his adventures. Each film could end with an engagement or a wedding.

In *Good Luck Russia*, the fantasy of marriage becomes more precise and more real, but remains a "super-marriage", that is to say a fiction in the eyes of the characters themselves. Indeed, if, more than in *James Bond vs. Doctor No*, we go from fantasy to a quasi-reality, the union between the British agent and the Russian corporal remains no less fictional. The romantic comedy of "overmarriage" is only a game to better appropriate a decoder that the Spectre organization covets. Tatiana Romanova and James Bond imagine putting a ring on their finger in order to pass themselves off as an English couple, Caroline and David Somerset.

The haunting of desire is strong in this film whose action takes place in the Balkans, in particular in the city of Istanbul, a dream city of espionage, cosmopolitan and full of mysteries, where we meet Soviets, Americans, Bulgarians, British, etc. Moreover, the model for this second part of 007's cinematographic adventures, which dates from 1963, is Alfred Hitchcock's film *Vertigo*, released in 1958.

In both cases, the urban setting plays an essential role, filmed in a surreal climate, a mysterious and dreamy atmosphere: San Francisco for *Vertigo*, Istanbul for *Greetings from Russia*. Thus in the scene of the saga that takes place inside the Christian basilica of Saint Sophia. Staring at the dome that rises fifty-five meters above the ground, the camera of *Good Kisses from Russia* captures the gigantism and the emptiness of the sacred place, where individuals seem tiny and distant. Only the voice of the guide resounds. Hitchcock also films the urban place, to capture its visual and dreamlike space-time, in its solemnity and eternity. Thus, in *Vertigo,* the Golden Gate Bridge, Lincoln Park or the Legion of Honor Museum. The couple of the two lovers James Bond and Tatiana Romanova resembles, to a certain extent, the Hitchcockian duo formed by Kim Novak and James Stewart in the cinematic fable that is *Vertigo*. The "over-marriage" in one, the themes of fantasy, haunting, illusion and simulacra in the other. Finally, one cannot but notice that another Hitchcock film serves as a reference to *Good Luck Russia*: the famous chase between Cary Grant and a plane, on a deserted field, in *North by Northwest* in 1959 inspires the scene where 007 is tracked by a helicopter, near the coast of Istria.

But for Bond, the romantic comedy becomes a tragic melodrama: while the "over-marriage" is usually fictitious, as a cover for the spies, Bond willingly lends himself to the game, and the break-up of the engagement becomes a pain for him: in *On ne vit que deux fois*, Bond is in perfect love with Aki, of the Japanese secret service. 007 hopes that Tigre Tanaka will agree to let his spy marry him for the needs of a mission. Alas, not only is Aki refused the role, but she dies during her night of love with Bond: as drops of poison drip down a wire hung by a Spectre agent over their bed to kill 007, Aki turns to her lover and swallows the poison in her sleep. Despite the grief, Bond continues his mission and plays the role of Kissy Suzuki's Japanese husband, during the traditional wedding ceremony in a temple, followed by a honeymoon on the small island Matsu where fishermen live.

Of course, the entire James Bond saga is built on the tragic and painful loss of Countess Teresa Di Vincenzo. In *Her Majesty's Secret Service*, Bond marries the daughter of the Corsican crime syndicate boss Marc-Ange Draco. In this film, unique in many ways, the "over-marriage" is an important part of the plot, before the wedding ceremony at the end. From the very beginning, when they first meet on the beach, the relationship between Teresa and James is a fairy tale romance. After rescuing her from the clutches of two assassins in pursuit, and as she disappears in a car, Bond finds himself alone on the beach with only the pair of shoes Teresa left behind. Classic image of Prince Charming and the princess in distress. Then, at the casino gambling table, when Teresa has just lost her card game, Bond reminds the croupier that he is teaming up with her and agrees to pay the debts of the one he doesn't really know yet. "Why are you trying so hard to help me?" the young woman asks. James Bond answers: "It's become a habit with me, Countess Teresa. And the intimacy between the two of them settles: "Teresa was a saint, she says, call me Tracy."

The classic figures of romance and old-fashioned chivalry are at the forefront of *In Her Majesty's Secret Service*: Bond courts "Tracy" by a fountain, surrounded by laughing birds and a black kitten. The two lovers barely touch hands, but exchange glances and conversations during long, intimate, shy moments: horseback riding, a bucolic stroll through a garden surrounded by Greco-Roman statues. Hand in hand, romantic tête-à-tête, a sunset beach getaway, shopping in town and strolling past a jeweler, a stroll through the zoo and playing with animals, Bond is a thoughtful, gallant and tender suitor.

A typical scene of this *new age* romance takes place during a car ride, in Marc-Ange Draco's Rolls-Royce Silver Shadow Drophead coupe. The three characters are in the back seat. In the middle of the seat, the father, a little grumpy and stubborn, but benevolent, turns his head alternately from right to left, looking successively at his son-in-law and his daughter who do not leave each other's eyes: they do not speak, but exchange words of love through their eyes. They smile at each other, they love each other. At this precise moment, the spectator is almost witnessing a kind of remake: the adolescent look of complicity between the two young lovers, who surround the father, recalls a scene from Stanley Donen's *Charade*, a film from 1963, while *On Her Majesty's Secret Service* dates from 1969: George Lazenby looks like Cary Grant, Diana Rigg has the features of Audrey Hepburn, Mrs. Lampert in *Charade*, and Marc-Ange Draco, played by Gabriele Ferzetti, looks like the actor Walter Matthau.

Another romantic scene shows James Bond ready to take the plunge and quit his job as a secret agent to get married. Because of a snowstorm, surrounded by bad weather, Bond and Tracy find refuge in a farm, a barn with hay, straw, animals. "I'm thinking of us," says 007. But "a secret agent can only be a lonely man," he says, his gaze lost in the distance, while Tracy looks down and their faces barely touch. "I should change my job, I love you, you are the woman of my life. Will you marry me?" declares Bond. "Mr. and Mrs. James Bond," he adds. And Tracy imagines herself already settled in a nice cottage: "Acacia Avenue, Tunbridge Wells. But Bond sees further afield: "Belgrave Square, or Paris, Monaco, Rome, or this barn!"

At their wedding in traditional costume, at the Portuguese estate of the bride's father, the Corsican godfather's thugs rub shoulders with the MI6 team, Moneypenny, M and Q. More romantic than ever, Bond cuts the cake, quotes poetry and throws his hat to the MI6 secretary, who is moved to tears. The "over-marriage" disappears for a moment: the fantasy has given way to reality, even if, as soon as they drive off in their "Just married" car, the two young spouses are planning to have three girls and three boys. "We have all eternity ahead of us!" exclaims a hero finally freed from his anxieties and fears. But the bullet that then kills Mrs. Bond, fired from the car driven by Ernst Stavro Blofeld, leaves a man alone on the side of the road, collapsed, desperate, shaking hands with his beloved wife and crying behind the veil that hides their faces.

Bond is inconsolable over Tracy's death. Many episodes evoke this impossible mourning. 007 will never be the same again: at the opening of the film *Just for Your Eyes*, James Bond pays his respects at his wife's grave and brings her an armful of red roses. On the grave, the following epitaph reads: "Terasa Bond, 1943-1969. Beloved wife of James Bond. We have all the time in the world." He then mourns his beloved deceased.

007 sometimes tries to recapture romantic moments, during delicious "over-wedding" rides in a horse-drawn carriage, under the snow with Melina Haveloch in Cortina d'Ampezzo - "Amore, amore" sings the coachman joyfully to them -, or with the Czech cellist Kara Milovy in the sunny streets of Vienna, waving to the artists and street musicians. But he remains deeply wounded and insensitive to happiness. In *Permit to Kill*, after the wedding of his friends, thinking of his dear and beloved murdered wife, Bond remains alone and refuses the gift offered by Della Leiter who questions her husband about this refusal. Felix Leiter replies, "He was married a long time ago." In *GoldenEye*, his former friend Alec Trevelyan and 006 colleague at MI6, who later becomes the terrorist Janus, cruelly reminds Bond of his deepest flaw: "I don't ask you if all the women who open their arms to you make you forget the one you failed to protect." This remark, made in order to hurt Bond's heart and further accentuate

his sick guilt, reinforces the link between surface eroticism and deep romance.

This intimate suffering and permanent pain, like an insurmountable wound, is also felt by Bond in *Casino Royale* at the death of Vesper Lynd, for whom he devotes a sincere and absolute love to the point of resigning from MI6. However, the romance between the two lovers also begins like a fairy tale. Recovering in front of a lake, Bond confides in the Treasury liaison officer in charge of the *Financial Action Task Force*: "I have no more armor, you've torn it off. Whatever is left of me, I belong to you." Kissing in the rain like two young lovers, lying on the beach in the sun or drifting off into the unknown on a sailboat, Vesper and 007 share a perfect love. On board the boat the *Spirit*, the young woman takes the helm while the man writes to M to give him his resignation "with immediate effect". Arrived in Venice, the couple does not miss any delicate attention towards each other. The "overmarriage" has already invested their relationship: not to be a woman maintained, Vesper announces to her fiancé that she wants to go immediately to the bank. "I want to pay half of our wanderings," she says. She shakes him out of the bed by throwing him a cushion: " Go! I'll take care of the money, you take care of the groceries." Again the "overmarriage", pure fantasy, seems to lead to a marriage well and truly real as the relationship between the two lovers resembles that of a normal couple, who share the household money and household decisions. But this quasi-reality is short-lived: the death of Vesper Lynd, drowned after the collapse of a Venetian palace, is a heartbreaker. The mysterious and dark woman dies underwater, trapped in the freight elevator. Melodrama and tragedy reinforce Bond's obsession with the vital need to marry. Inconsolable and pursued by his own anxieties and inner demons, Bond is a lonely man. No woman can ever bring him happiness. None, really?

Miracle in London

The only female figure with whom the lover will never dare to take the plunge, nor declare his love, Eve Moneypenny is nevertheless the woman of his life. If Miss Moneypenny is entitled to a simple "Ciao" in *James Bond vs. Doctor No*, tenderness is the order of the day in *Good Luck Russia*: "Ah, the Bosphorus in the moonlight...", Bond sighs, cheek to cheek, with M's secretary at MI6. "Take me away sometime," she tells him. "As the woman of my life, I only recognize you," says 007. The dialogue between Moneypenny and Bond continues independently from film to film. A secret intimacy gradually develops between them, in the antechamber of the plot and the action: Moneypenny's office, located just before M's, both spatially and temporally. It is a closed and discreet place, out of sight and ideal for courting. Protected by this private wall that separates him from the rest of the world, Bond is himself, authentic. With Miss Moneypenny, he leaves behind the dandy seducer's panoply to become a simple, delicate and thoughtful man. And to Bond's statement, made in *Good Kisses from Russia* with humor and in a flirtatious tone, Moneypenny seems to answer in *Goldfinger*: "The gold I know is the one worn on the ring finger," Moneypenny announces, adding: "Come to dinner at my place, on the menu: coq en pâte."

If the dinner does not take place, the discussion is never interrupted between the two characters from 1962 to 2020: in *On ne vit que deux fois*, Bond's colleague trains him to pronounce the password for his future mission in Japan: "You will say it without difficulty: 'I love you. Please repeat it aloud to me!'" If seduction is the order of the day, Bond can count on Moneypenny in hard times. If she reproaches him for not even sending a postcard, in *On Her Majesty's Secret Service, a* few moments later, when M has just taken away the Bedlam operation, Bond angrily dictates his letter of resignation to Moneypenny. But the secretary, without warning him, replaces "resignation" with "request for a fortnight's leave".

The verbal jousting, jubilant and seductive, seems to create a particular attachment and a unique complicity as the adventures progress. Isn't the spectator himself under the spell of this recreational frolic and this vacation childishness? The regularity of their relationship brings Bond a beneficial stability and Moneypenny a momentary entertainment. Is there anything else to it? When she hands him the fake passport in the name of Peter Franks to follow up on a diamond deal in *Diamonds Are Forever*, Bond gives her a friendly poke, no doubt already knowing her reaction: "What can I bring you back from Holland? She seizes the opportunity: "A diamond? On a ring?", but Bond doesn't stop there: "How about a tulip!"

While respecting this relationship of love complicity or simple game, Moneypenny is however there to support the MI6 agent. She helps him, in delicate missions, in particular with regard to the hierarchy of 007. Little concerned with protocol, Bond has the support of his girlfriend who, after having participated herself in a subterfuge in *Live and Let Die*, does not fail to remind him this one - "Goodbye James, or should I say *ciao bello*?" - while M is about to discover the Italian spy "Mademoiselle Caruso" in a closet of 007's London apartment.

But can genuine tenderness and delicate attention, as when Bond gives her a white rose in *Nothing But Your Eyes* and a light kiss on the cheek, lead the two friends to a more carnal and sensual relationship? In *Killing is Not Playing*, an invitation to come and listen to music at her house causes trouble. And when 007 is nowhere to be found in *Licence to Kill*, M's secretary worries. Not having heard from James Bond, she makes five spelling mistakes on the first page of the document M asks her to write. More serene and direct, Moneypenny makes fun of 007's excesses: "I could sue you for sexual harassment," she says in *GoldenEye*, before giving him a bit of a lecture in *Tomorrow Never Dies*: "Queen and country James!" Moneypenny also has an answer and does not let Bond lead the seduction game alone. "You brought me a souvenir from your trip? Chocolates? An engagement ring?" she banters to titillate him in *The World is Not Enough*, before throwing away the cigar case he hands her. But Bond adds, not to lose the hand in this game of face-to-face: "Moneypenny, this is the image of our relationship, you reject all my advances."

Sex comes to fill in or interrupt the love game for a moment, in the form of a virtual simulation: at the end of *Die Another Day*, Moneypenny fantasizes about an erotic relationship with Bond with the help of three-dimensional glasses in Q's laboratory. Then, in *Skyfall*, if we follow the cinematic order, their relationship takes another turn: Moneypenny, originally a field agent on a mission to Istanbul to retrieve the list of NATO double agents infiltrating terrorist organizations, unwittingly shoots Bond. Bond confronts Patrice, Silva's killer, on a speeding train. Moneypenny's bullet hits Bond, who falls into the water. This field relationship continues and strengthens, despite 007's injury caused by his colleague.

Another scene in *Skyfall* evokes, in an implied way, a dreamed "over-marriage" between the two characters. Coming to visit her hotel room, Moneypenny notices the traditional barber's razor that 007 possesses. This last takes advantage of it to declare her half-wordly his love: " I make some things in the old way ". She answers him: "The old methods are sometimes the best. Are they talking about espionage or marriage, work or feelings? Perhaps they are simply talking about the distinction between razor blades and electric razors.

The couple share other novel experiences, for example when Moneypenny accompanies Bond to the casino in Macau. Faced with Silva's men, the spy falls into a pit filled with Komodo dragons. Moneypenny then pulls him out of this bad situation and helps 007 to get out of reach of these ferocious animals. And it is Moneypenny again who gives 007 a horrible little porcelain bulldog, draped in the British flag, a gift from M written in his will. If Bond, in *Spectre*, allows himself to telephone Moneypenny in the middle of the night, or to ask her to be a mole for him in the new intelligence service, a merger of MI5 and MI6 coordinated by Max Denbigh - whom 007 decides to call C out of mockery - it is because the only person James Bond trusts, the only person he can count on, in sixty years of adventures and actions, is Moneypenny, the only woman Bond has ever loved.

She has elegance and restraint, charm and distinction, refinement and courtesy. And James Bond can only desire her without ever possessing her because she will always remain for him an inaccessible fantasy. But yes, but it is of course! Wouldn't Miss Moneypenny be, in reality, the Queen Mother Elizabeth II of England and the Commonwealth? This sensational revelation is a rudely well kept secret. The love between Eve and James is, in the end, a love talk, made of words, sweet bills or exchanged words. This verbal and non-carnal relationship is part of a long aesthetic tradition expressing thwarted desire. The eternal complicity between the two MI6 agents is at the crossroads of three literary genres: first, impossible and forbidden love, as in the passion between Delphine d'Albémar and Léonce de Mondoville, in Madame de Staël. Then the courtly and gallant love, like the adventures which bind Érec and Énide, in the work of Chrétien de Troyes. Finally, platonic and chaste love, in the manner of Erika Ewald and the virtuoso violinist, a young man whose name is unknown, in Stefan Zweig's short story. A new duo like Romeo and Juliet, Eve and James find themselves in the firmament of the stars living a crazy, fantasized and unrealizable love.

4. FROM THE GLORIOUS BODY TO THE SPECTRAL BODY, THE RESURRECTION OF THE GHOST

The perception of the sensible allows us to see James Bond from his body and his flesh. A philosophical breakthrough right under the hero's skin allows us to draw out a spectral phenomenology of his being-in-the-world. Beyond life and death, what kind of survival is 007's existence? How to approach the plasticity of his carnal envelope? In other words, is James Bond a classic superhero, insensitive to the effects of time as well as to the marks of blows or violence on his body?

The force is with him

In the age of superheroes, many modern-day hercules populate our imagination. Some are incredibly powerful, like the Titans or the Asgardians like Thor. Others possess unsuspected physical resources, like Ethan Hunt and the members of the Mission Impossible Force. Others, in this race for the most spectacular feat, and perhaps to give themselves courage or to have a famous "ancestor" in their pantheon, bear in their name the well-known initials of a British agent, like the investigator of the American anti-terrorist cell CTU Jack Bauer (*JB*) or the CIA agent Jason Bourne (*JB*). In all cases, regardless of the surname, the invincibility overkill is the order of the day.

007 does not escape the rule. His animal and bestial body, his instinctive intelligence and his fast reflexes give him a definite advantage over his opponents. The force is, without a doubt, with him. But how much energy does our hero have? James Bond's vitality is not just his physical power, static and all muscle. On the contrary, 007 deploys an aesthetic of virtuosity and a choreography of agility.

From this point of view, the films of the 007 saga form a metaphysical ballet. Like a flamboyant faun, emerging from an ancient bas-relief, James Bond has the suppleness of the feline and the vibration of the Sphinx. A kind of swirling energy of which only certain virtuoso dancers are capable. Cadence, measure, rhythm and tempo are revealed through him. This form of inner energy, lively and fast, and this formidable capacity to adapt to circumstances and events, allow him to escape the most difficult traps.

As such, one of the most spectacular running chases in cinema can be found in *Skyfall.*

If we see a wild fight between a cobra and a mongoose, the savagery only gets stronger: backpacking, the saboteur and bomb maker named Mollaka is an outstanding *free-runner* and climber. Using only the speed of his legs and his body balance, he tries to lose 007 through a construction site and a building under construction. Jostling the workers, he makes multiple dizzying jumps and perilous climbs. James Bond is not to be outdone: he climbs, runs, leaps and climbs cranes and elevators with the strength of his arms alone. Jumping from one platform to another above the void, he catches up with his opponent and confronts him with his bare hands at the top of a crane. Succeeding in escaping 007, Mollaka walks along the beams of the building site to reach the nearby street. Still pursued by the British agent, he tries to return to the Nambutu embassy in Madagascar. On his side, Bond, suspended from a cable, jumps directly onto the sidewalk and over the barbed wire. He enters the embassy, takes Mollaka hostage, and eliminates a dozen military guards from the diplomatic security. James Bond shows impressive physical and mental strength in a race against time. The baroque orchestration of this scene is breathtaking, allowing 007 to access the "ELLIPSIS" code on his adversary's laptop recovered from his enemy's backpack.

Already in *James Bond vs. Doctor No*, the hero shows a keen sense of improvisation in the face of the unpredictable: in the swamps, in the middle of a river, Bond, Quarrell and Honey Rider are surrounded by armed guards and accompanied by dogs. 007 has the wit to quickly cut some reed, discovered by chance in the ferns, in order to improvise stems allowing to breathe under water and to hide there, putting himself, as well as his friends, in the shelter.

When he confronts a colossus, 007 deploys a choreography of agile boxer or Greco-Roman wrestler. Tensed, violated, moved and hit, the real body is strongly solicited. Whirling and twirling 007 is on the ring. The wrestler rushes forward and unleashes his blows.

In the form of head-to-head, hand-to-hand or face-to-face, the films of the 007 saga reinvent the modern duel. Two opponents, one against the other, ready to do anything to overcome, surpass and destabilize their opponent.

The giant and behemoth Hinx, henchman of Franz Oberhauser - James Bond's adopted brother who is none other than Ernst Stavro Blofeld - confronts 007 in the restaurant car and kitchens of a train taking them to the Sahara desert. In this scene of *Spectre*, the violence of the blows and the power of the muscles almost destroy the car. *In extremis,* Madeleine

Swann and James Bond manage to tie a knot around Hinx's massive neck, and tie the rope to various barrels and casks in order to throw the killer out of the train.

Faced with a veritable "ice-cream cabinet", the Spectre's killer Donald Grant in *From Russia with Love,* Bond also has to deploy intense and concentrated energy, as the space of their fight is so small: the room of a sleeper car on the Orient Express train to Trieste, after Grant has impersonated Captain Nash in Zagreb. 007 manages to divert his attention by setting off a tear gas canister. But the hand-to-hand fight in the car leads Bond to strangle his enemy with the cord of his watch, ending a grueling and violent hand-to-hand battle.

Bond's body is glorious in that it sublimates the environment around it to gain the upper hand. Locked in a barred cage, even if that cage is a giant vault, the basement of the gold reserves of Fort Knox, Bond finds himself facing the dumb and tough Korean killer Oddjob. The battle between the two men is unequal, between body mass on one side and physical agility on the other. Bond grabs anything he can find around him - a metal bar, a gold bar - to destabilize his opponent. But, impassive, even smiling at his enemy, Oddjob does not bother to dodge the attacks. The blows do nothing to him, he feels no pain. He walks, slowly, while Bond multiplies his movements and attempts. The epic battle suddenly turns upside down. Taking hold of his enemy's metal-brimmed hat, Bond aims but misses Oddjob, who moves towards the hat to retrieve it. At that very moment, 007 grabs a cable which, placed against the bars, electrocutes Oddjob, causing a deluge of light, explosions and fireworks.

There is an immanent jubilation, for the spectator, to observe James Bond in a bad position, facing beings that are disproportionate and out of the norm by their cruelty, by their size, by their inhumanity. A merciless struggle is then played out, but it is first and foremost an ancient spectacle in a Greek amphitheater. The pre-generic of *Operation Thunder* puts in scene 007 with the colonel Jacques Bouvard, number 6 of the Spectre, in a rough and testing hand-to-hand fight. If the duel uses here many pieces of antiquity as weapons of combat, it finishes by a strangulation with the handle of a firebrand, in front of an old chimney. Each duel is an arena fight, each attack is a confrontation with a gladiator. James Bond is a kind of "revolted man", as defined by Albert Camus. To overcome the traps and defeat his enemies, 007 has no choice but to engage in a spontaneous movement to overcome his condition, like the ancient hero Spartacus, the rebellious slave who shook the power of the Roman Empire, a political organization as formidable as the Spectre. Although every hero has his own battle cry, 007 could take up the battle cry of the rebellious gladiator, and say, in the manner of the late Kirk Douglas who embodied him in Stanley Kubrick's film, "I am Spartacus."

The physical fight is a habit in the body duels of the films of the saga. But what matters, in the end, is the spectacular dimension of the fight. Without accessories, neither mask nor cothurn: only the body is at stake. Caught in an in-between situation, the spectator hesitates and gropes, torn between the ignoble cruelty and the marvelous entertainment. The world of James Bond is that of Homeric fabulation ending in Latin triumph.

If James Bond faces the most diabolical Titans, from Tee Hee to Stamper, true psychopathic athletes, his worst adversary, or at least one of 007's most indestructible enemies, is the giant of about two meters named Jaws. Almost invincible, his artificial jaw with metallic teeth is deadly. His first appearance is chilling: he appears in the shadow of a pyramid, on the Giza plateau in Egypt, illuminated during a sound and light show. His shadow first gives him the appearance of a mummy, outside the tomb of Cheops, then that of a vampire when, inside the room of the dead, he kills Aziz Fekkesh with a bite in the neck. Later, in the same film, Jaws appears tiny in the background of a wide frame that reveals the immensity of the columns of an Egyptian temple. But make no mistake, Jaws is capable of stopping or cutting the cable of a gondola and confronting Bond on the roof of a cable car in Rio de Janeiro with his jaw.

Each situation of fight and confrontation forces 007 to reinvent himself unceasingly. He cannot remain on his assets and has to show more and more courage as the danger diversifies and multiplies. Faced with Colonel Rosa Klebb, former head of Smersh operations and now the Spectre's number 3, Bond dances with both a wild beast and a deadly insect. Armed only with a chair, 007 tries to fend off the colonel who has pulled out her stinger, a poisoned blade at the end of her shoe. The animal is violent, the venom-infected spur threatening to pierce Bond's leg with every blow. After successfully subduing the beast, 007 has a little fun: "She was dancing on her toes too much." On the Octopussy train, twins Mischka and Grishka are knife throwers who once murdered a Bond colleague, 009, in East Berlin. They face 007 in an epic duel. A more aerial battle pits James Bond against Necros, a chameleon-killer - he disguises himself as a milkman, a jogger or a doctor - and a music lover - he never leaves his walkman, always listens to the same music, and uses the headphone cable of his portable audio player to strangle his victims. Suspended in the air and hanging simply from a net over the mountains of Afghanistan, Bond and Necros fight in the back of a sinking plane that is open to the air. To get rid of his opponent, Bond cuts the laces of his own shoe, to which his enemy was clinging, sending Necros into limbo.

The physical effort is redoubled and accentuated during spectacular stunts and twists on skis, during terrible chases in the snow. Chased by Yamaha XJ 500 snowmobiles equipped with machine guns, pursued by KGB agent Erich Kriegler, Bond performs feats of strength to escape from them. From episode to episode, 007 multiplies his efforts in sensational exercises, worthy of a high-speed aerobatics.

Sometimes Bond finds himself up against seasoned gymnasts. He faces Olympic-level opponents and athletes like

Bambi and Thumper in a fight where they try to strangle him with their legs. Only a supple and moving body can defeat his enemies in this type of confrontation. 007 must work and maintain his body to acquire the necessary flexibility and acrobatic dexterity, in order to get out of the clutches of opponents as tough as powerful.

In his aikido outfit, Hugo Drax's hitman Chang is armed with the *jo*, a martial arts staff, and a *katana*, the samurai sword. He violently confronts Bond in the ancient museum of the glassmaker Venini, in Venice, then in the Torre dell'Orologio of the city. As 007 carries in his pocket a sample of a deadly gas he wants to have analyzed, contained in a simple test tube, the fight rages on: protected by a mesh mask, Chang strikes forcefully in front of him, without paying attention to the precious porcelain around him. Bond is trying to protect a cup made in 1520 and worth a million dollars. Faced with the sharp blade of his opponent's Japanese *katana,* Bond grabs a sword belonging to General Menotti dating from the late 18th century. But Bond is a master in the art of foil and sword. He also shows his fencing skills in *Die Another Day*: after initial training with Verity, Bond takes on the best foil in the London club, Gustav Graves, at a thousand pounds a hit. "En garde!", Bond announces in French, before betting the outcome of the fight with Cuban diamonds.

Another place, another scene, another opponent. In the crowded streets of New Delhi, during a chase in a *tuk-tuk* cab, Gobinda tries to kill Bond with a blunderbuss, after having demonstrated his physical strength during a game of backgammon between the spy and the Afghan prince Kamal Khan: Gobinda is a tall Sikh in traditional costume and turban. Staring straight at Bond in the games, he crushes the game's loaded dice with the strength of his one hand. In a breathtaking epic scene, Bond confronts Gobinda with his bare hands in an aerial battle. Several hundred feet above the ground, the two men fight on the roof of a speeding Beech 18 aircraft.

James Bond does not only face human beings, but also a formidable bestiary, sometimes imaginary (the dragon on the island of Doctor No, which frightens the population with its burning breath and shining eyes - it is actually a machine with a diesel engine and blinding headlights), but most of the time real and dangerous. From the black widow, a spider with deadly venom that crawls up his leg in *James Bond vs. Doctor No*, to the scorpion on his arm while he's drinking his ass off in a bar in *Skyfall,* the animals are challenges to 007's Herculean strength. Faced with sharks in Emilio Largo's Palmyra estate; faced with old Albert, the crocodile that took Tee Hee's right arm - "Well done Albert! "and his fellow alligators of the Louisiana bayou; underwater against a gigantic green anaconda at the entrance of an Inca temple, at the end of the Tiparare River, in the Amazoco area; facing the symbolic octopus, emblem of the Spectre organization.

But sometimes James Bond himself is disguised as an animal: with a fake seabird on his head, as he swims in a suit to blow up Ramirez's drug refinery, in *Goldfinger*; or moving as a fake crocodile in the water, to get to the floating palace in Octopussy.

007 is a man whose body is abused and submitted to harsh tests. Drugged, choked, asphyxiated, burned or chained, 007 survives and overcomes the worst situations. Many scenes of the saga show a hero exposed to mental and physical torture. He is victim of atrocious sufferings. Subjected to Goldfinger's laser beam, a luminous filter capable of splitting wood or metal, Bond has to show an impressive coolness and an efficient bluff to convince his enemy to stop his infernal machine, to leave 007 alive and to keep him as a precious hostage.

In the Tower of Leander or the Tower of the Virgin in Istanbul, Elektra King wants to have fun torturing her prisoner. She ties 007 on an antique torture chair, a real infernal machine and strangulation device. "Don't you find that traditions are lost?", she tells him, by cruel game and sadism. But the longest torture inflicted on the British agent is the one he undergoes during his capture for fourteen months, in North Korean jails. On the coast of Pukch'ŏng, Bond, long hair and shaggy beard, continues to joke with his tormentors and torturers. "Talk to my janitor!" he replies to them.

With his extraordinary control and calmness, Bond is subjected to the worst treatment, brutality, outrages and abuse. Could he be insensitive to pain? In a dark dungeon, he is able to laugh as Le Chiffre tortures him with infinite cruelty. How can he resist such violence inflicted upon him? Completely naked, tied and chained to a chair, Bond is manhandled by the killer, who hits his genitals with a rope knot. Bond screams, suffers, moans and struggles with all his might, facing a sick and perverted being. Le Chiffre does not leave his inhaler. He has a scar on his left eye and a disorder of the lacrimal glands makes him cry blood. Without feeling any compassion for his victim, Le Chiffre physically tortures 007 to obtain the passwords that will allow him to recover the money won at the casino by the spy. The latter finds the strength to resist his tormentor. He throws him a line of humor: "The whole world will know that you are dead by scratching my balls!"

Another torture scene shows Bond tied to a chair with his wrists bound with a strap. In front of the imprisoned Madeleine Swann, who is watching the session, Franz Oberhauser reveals to 007 that he is the leader of a worldwide terrorist organization called "Spectre" and that his name is Ernst Stavro Blofeld. The angora cat climbs onto Bond's lap and he is tortured, first mentally: Blofeld reveals to him that he is the murderer of his adoptive father. Blofeld's father adopted the young orphan James Bond and helped him overcome the disappearance of his parents, who died in a mountaineering accident. He taught him to ski, climb and hunt. But Blofeld killed his own father, making it look like an avalanche in the mountains, leaving Bond without a family again.

While recounting these events of the past, the Spectre's leader manipulates a computer to insert a syringe or needle into Bond's skull, which makes him scream in pain.

How then does one and the same individual, 007, manage to survive so much violence and to overcome so many missions, each more dangerous and perilous than the last? If his body is constantly abused, is James Bond a superhuman in the sense of Nietzsche? Being one with the organs of his body, the spirit of the superhuman is able to intensify his existence, to create new values in his life and to overcome the destructive nihilism that surrounds him. The Nietzschean Bond succeeds in rising above human brutality and barbarism in order to overcome himself.

Such is the fourth secret of James Bond: faced with the death that threatens him and sometimes reaches him, 007 seems to return unceasingly from the realm of the dead. Like a spectre or a ghost, but carried by the values of becoming, he embodies the thought of the eternal return. Faced with the destructive spiral of nihilism, in the violent world of espionage, 007 makes of the repetition a will to live again. "Live and let die", "Die" is not enough and "Die" can wait: carried by such a will to live again, 007 makes of the infinite repetition of his missions, sign of his return and his resurrection, a thought of love. Life against death, affirmation against negation, will against despair. In each film, James Bond appears as a new Heracles, Orpheus or Aeneas: he challenges the Underworld, but with a particularity that the heroes of mythology do not possess. If 007 accepts to cross the Tartarus or is ready to cross the Styx, he will do it in a hang glider or a speedboat.

Moreover, for Nietzsche, only the nomad, the adventurer or the explorer is capable of living without bondage and of asserting a genuine courage to overcome all trials. One gets the impression that Bond corresponds to this definition given by Nietzsche in *Le gai savoir*: "Trained as he is to stand on ropes and even to dance to the edge of abysses, such a spirit would be the free spirit par excellence."

Dead spy walking

"Look at him!" announces Damian Falco, the head of the NSA, to his staff as a shadowy figure emerges, like a hallucination, "he almost looks like a hero." As he says these words, we can make out a silhouette advancing through the mist, on the bridge between North and South Korea, for an exchange between two prisoners in *Die Another Day*. Like a ghost with long hair and a full beard, dressed in rags, Bond is an indistinct form that slowly appears in the fog. Half dead, half alive, he looks like a ghost from beyond the grave and from the dead. Elektra King is right to ask him this question in *The World Is Not Enough*: "How do you survive?" James Bond gives him this Nietzschean answer: "I revel in the beauty of the world.

One of the most surprising characteristics of the James Bond saga is that the hero has several burials, several deaths and therefore also several rebirths. He is not a superhero but a superhuman. If he is an over-trained man of action and fieldwork, Bond is ultimately a mortal being, in the true sense of the word, even a dying one, but capable of overcoming this finitude and overcoming this contingency. This is Bond's metaphysics, his profound ontology.

How many times does James Bond die before rising from his ashes? He dies several times, but each time with a different tombstone. James Bond is not an immortal superhero, but he dies often and therefore has nine lives, like Blofeld's cat.

Are we, as spectators, victims of a hallucination on the screen, of a subjective vision of the image? An ectoplasmic figure or a corporeal spectre, Bond appears to our philoscopic gaze as an interstitial being, a figure of passage or interval, who never dies and never lives either, but *survives* in an unreal way. Prestidigitation seems to be a recurrent cinematographic exercise, an artistic phenomenon capable of playing on the onirism of 007. Between appearances and disappearances, 007 is the phoenix of the espionage, the firebird of the secret services.

Is it an aesthetic of the marvelous or the fantastic that makes us see Bond dead everywhere and alive again each time? There is a disturbance in the materiality of his body, which goes from real or glorious to spectral or ghostly. What does this mean? Bond is a being of emergence, of appearance, of suddenness. His temporality is not linear, but cyclical. His existence is not built on longevity, but on instantaneity.

Demonic and angelic, half-dead and half-alive, half-reflection and half-shadow, Bond lives between two worlds. An individual at once natural and artificial, the materiality of his being is not only made of flesh and blood, but it seems of another order: polymorphic, hybrid, multiple, heterogeneous and machine-like. A fluid and translucent figure, 007 is a spectral figure of MI6. If he only consumes vodka Martini, a fuel not officially approved by MI6, this cocktail apparently allows Bond to function without regularly recharging his batteries.

But why say that Bond dies indefinitely? All the films give us the answer.

The pre-credits of *Good Luck Russia* follow Donald Grant, in the middle of the night in the garden of an estate with ancient statues, on Spectre Island. He is about to murder someone. In less than two minutes he kills James Bond, before the lights come on in the estate and the spectators of the scene congratulate Grant for killing a fake James Bond. Even though the victim was wearing a mask that had 007's face and features, the imposture and deception may have been an illusion for a moment.

The illusion of Bond's death resurfaces in the opening scene of *Operation Thunder*: the film opens with a funeral scene, which makes us believe in the possible or probable death of the British agent. A religious ceremony takes place in a church. A priest, surrounded by altar boys, says a prayer around a mortuary coffin on which are inscribed the initials "JB". For a few moments the spectator imagines of course that 007 has passed from life to death, before seeing the hero on the balcony. Accompanied by a French Bureau official, Bond is actually attending the funeral of Jacques Bouvard, who is responsible for the deaths of two of his MI6 colleagues. A moment later, a mistake made by Bouvard allows 007 to understand that it is also a decoy: Bouvard is not dead but, disguised as a black widow, he is in mourning for his own funeral. Bond has just unmasked him.

We only live twice opens with the assassination of 007, killed in his bed in Hong Kong. In reality, once again an illusion: the secret agent simulates his own death. He was not killed, but a staging must make believe in his fatal disappearance : 007's funeral is announced on the front page of the newspapers. The press makes its headlines: "British Commander Murdered". To give the change and maintain this false death, the funeral takes place in the middle of the sea, celebrated from the ship *HMS Tenby*. A speech in honor of the deceased hero was given in front of all the sailors. The song of the dead resounds: "The trumpets shall sound, and the dead shall rise." With the body thrown into the water, the water coffin is retrieved by two divers in scuba suits, who transport the human sarcophagus to a secret MI6 underwater base. Once the bandages are removed, Bond humorously asks, "May I come aboard?" And Moneypenny, present, adds, "Always late James, even to your own funeral."

In *Her Majesty's Secret Service,* a particularly strong visual scene takes place in the middle of the mountains. Blofeld and his men trigger a terrible avalanche. Following the detonation of explosive rockets, a deluge of snow falls and carries away everything in its path: trees torn up, rocks shattered, stones displaced. Launched at full speed, the heaps of white powder engulf Tracy Di Vicenzo and James Bond who disappear under a cataclysmic cloud. The two bodies seem inert, immobile under a ton of snow. Satisfied, Blofeld concludes, "007 has finally gone down to the grave." Was the spy killed in the avalanche, as were his parents and his adoptive father? The next shot shows James Bond in a window frame. He is in London, closing his eyes. In the frame of this window appears in superposition or superimposition the movement of Tracy's body, carried away by Blofeld's men. Then a phone call interrupts this sad and dreamlike thought. Is the death dreamed, imagined, or did it really happen?

In *Diamonds Are Forever*, 007 is constantly confronted with his own death. First in Amsterdam, where he poses as diamond dealer Peter Franks, a gem transport consultant. But when he meets the real Peter Franks in the old elevator shaft of Tiffany Case's Dutch building, Bond finally gets rid of this troublesome double. But, to give the change to the young woman and to know where are hidden the fifty thousand carats, 007 exchanges his wallet with the one he has just cooled. Tiffany Case exclaims, by discovering the false identity of the corpse: "You have just killed James Bond!" And 007 adds: "Like nobody is indestructible."

In Las Vegas, where he arrived a little later in the same film, Bond goes to the Morton Slumber Funeral Home to make the exchange between the diamonds and the money. Inside the funeral home, the stained glass window of this Nevada church is shaped like a diamond. But Bond is knocked out by Wint and Kidd. The two killers lock the unconscious spy's body in a coffin to be cremated and burned to ashes. Trapped, Bond finds himself at his own funeral in Las Vegas, before the mortician stops the cremation: "These diamonds are fake!", the one who has just interrupted Bond's transformation into dust throws at him. 007 reacts immediately: "Don't say anything, are you St. Peter?"

In New Orleans, in *Live and Let Die* the real murders are multiplied during fake funeral processions. On the street, on two occasions, investigators are murdered while looking for leads on the mysterious Dr. Kananga, Prime Minister of the Caribbean island of San Monica. While watching the Fillet of Soul restaurant out of the corner of his eye, Liaison Officer Hamilton asks who is being buried as the grieving family and the *Brass Band* play a funeral march for the death ceremony as they pass by on the street. One of the Kananga killers replied, "Your funeral," before killing him and making his body disappear in the coffin. The same tragic end for CIA agent Harold Strutter, who dies in the same way: the fake funeral procession becomes his own, in the same place, shortly afterwards. But what about Bond? Is he too attending his own funeral? Just before destroying the acres of poppy fields cultivated by Kananga with programmed firebombs, 007 comes to rescue Solitaire tied to a pole during a ritual voodoo ceremony. During the satanic trance and the wild dances, one of the inhabitants of San Monique puts a feathered hat on a grave, and gives machete blows, to call Baron Samedi, skeleton man and god of the cemeteries. At that very moment, the viewer can read, on the tombstone, the name of the dead man: "In Loving Memory of James Brocket." This James Brocket, "JB", is he not again a double, a reflection of James Bond?

In the training room of his island paradise, Francisco Scaramanga has reconstructed a real carnival to practice shooting, with mannequins, virtual screens and false doors. Everything is illusion and appearance in this playful labyrinth that recalls the famous scene called "Mirror Maze" from Charlie Chaplin's 1928 film *The Circus.* When Tramp is chased, he finds himself in a corridor of mirrors where bodies are endlessly reproduced, as in the spirit of Scaramanga's carnival, where trompe-l'oeil, artifice and pretense reign. The whole of this playful device is controlled on computer by his butler Tric-Trac. Between a wax figure of Al Capone, a skeleton and fake western cowboys in a saloon, a trompe-l'oeil mirror and light panels, Nick Nack has installed for his master a life-size reproduction of the secret agent 007. At the end of his training, the professional shooter aims and shoots the four fingers of James Bond's left hand, or rather his wax double. As if the hero was accompanied by the image of his double. However, this is an unequal twin: if there are two Bonds, one is made of flesh and bone, the other is spectral and unreal.

Also in *The Man with the Golden Gun*, M receives a golden bullet engraved with the number 007 at the MI6 office. James

Bond wonders: "Who would want to kill me? His secret service boss replies, with a touch of sarcasm, "Jealous husbands, offended cooks, humiliated tailors." But when Bond faces Scaramanga, for the final duel refereed in French by Tric-Trac, 007 manages to trick the killer's vigilance by putting himself in the place of his own statue, in Scaramanga's morbid merry-go-round or theme park. Face to face with his life-size effigy, Bond puts himself in the place of his reproduction. He is therefore more real than life. In the fairy-tale world of cinema, is not everything an illusion and a set, a game of mirrors and pasteboard, a false image and a real artifice?

Simulated or fantasized, played out or announced, Bond's death is on everyone's lips. His former 006 colleague Alec Trevelyan, now the terrorist Janus, has already made the announcement: "Mr. Bond will have a modest funeral, escorted by Moneypenny and a few grieving restaurateurs." For his part, Elliot Carver is already declaring, through the television media he owns, "the death of a man unknown to the Hamburg police, who killed himself under unknown circumstances." This is of course Bond. Besides, the killer and forensic expert sent by Carver, Dr. Kaufman, is there to carry out what is already on the television screens.

But beyond fictional deaths, Bond also regularly comes back to life, literally. In *Die Another Day*, he has a cardiac arrest, passing from life to death. His electrocardiogram shows no heart activity and the doctors decide to inject him with atrophine to revive him. In *Casino Royale*, poisoned by his cocktail, Bond rushes to his car to find a syringe of counter-poison or electrodes. In the earpiece, MI6 tells him, "You'll be dead in less than two minutes unless you listen to me." Bond, nearly unconscious and on the verge of fainting, replies, "I'm all ears." With the help of a defibrillator, Versper Lynd first tries to bring 007 back to life. Then she perseveres and revives Bond with a dose of lidocaine and an electrode that brings him out of his ventricular and arrhythmic tachycardia.

Between death and resurrection, 007 plays a new game, that of the Freudian *fort-da*, also called "the game of the reel". Bond's game of "leaving-returning" becomes that of "disappearing-reappearing". Like the knight Antonius Blok in Ingmar Bergman's *The Seventh Seal*, Bond plays a game of chess with Death. And this game also involves M in *Skyfall*. In London, at MI6, 007's boss is writing her agent's death certificate; on her computer she writes his obituary: "Bond is presumed dead on a mission in Turkey." Back in her private apartment, M notices a shadow near the window. She recognizes the man who has just been resurrected: "Where the hell have you been? Bond replies, "I've been enjoying death."

Prisoner and tied up hand and foot in front of Silva, on the latter's desert island, in *Skyfall*, 007 tries to put on a brave face in front of the cyber-terrorist's intimidation. Bond tells him: "To each his own. The criminal then asks him: "What's yours?" And 007 replies, "Resurrection.

The next episode, aptly named *Spectre*, is understood in both senses of the word. The acronym refers to the international terrorist organization that specializes in murder, hijacking, kidnapping and political pressure. But it also refers to Bond himself, a true reflection of death among the living.

In fact, the opening of the film shows this perfectly. The pre-credits, for the first time, display a meaningful quote on the screen: "The dead are alive. ("The dead are alive.") On a mission to Mexico City during the Festival of the Dead, James Bond is dressed entirely as a skeleton. Wearing a black top hat and carrying a knobbed cane, 007, with his girlfriend of the day on his arm, enters the Dia de Muertos, a hotel, during the Zócalo festival.

Bond is dead in his own way in the midst of this alliance between party and murder, lightness and gravity, life and death. If the pre-credits or opening scene of *Spectre* celebrates a party, with costumes, dances and music, James Bond is a dead man on borrowed time. The title of the twenty-fifth film in the saga, *Dying Can Wait*, means, once again, that, for Agent 007, death is never far away. One of the last scenes of *Spectre* brings Bond back to the old SIS building, the destroyed MI6 headquarters, in southwest London, on the right bank of the Thames. In this burned-out *Legoland*, or Babylon, Bond reads on the wall the memorial plaque to MI6's fallen heroes: "In memory of those who died, in the service of their country." And, at the very bottom of the list, under the engraved names, is added to the tag or graffiti, that of "James Bond," in blood-red color, with an arrow on the left, pointing underground, to the entrance of the Styx and the Underworld.

At the heart of this metaphysical representation of death and life, 007 undertakes a chase with the Grim Reaper. Subject to strange metamorphoses, sometimes disappearing, sometimes reappearing, sometimes present, sometimes absent, sometimes visible, sometimes invisible, Bond is neither completely dead nor completely alive. Is Her Majesty's secret agent a fleeting illusion, a pure ectoplasm? If he is regularly called upon to descend to the grave, this ghostly image that haunts him adds to the psychology of the hero. Bond is a paranoid character, perpetually worried about his personal identity. When he meets Dr. Madeleine Swann, the Pale King's daughter, in the Hoffler Clinic, the Oxford and Sorbonne psychologist questions Bond about the trauma of his past and the wounds of his childhood. Bond confesses to her, half-heartedly, that he would need psychoanalysis to heal the unreal simulacra in which he lives. The nature of 007's body, both reflected and reflecting, is more invisible than invincible.

Supernatural or spectral being, 007 vanishes and disappears before being reborn and coming back. This existence of a being who comes back and of a figure who haunts those he meets, annoys strongly 007's opponents. Despite his apparent calm, the cruel psychopath Hugo Drax gradually shows his irritation: "James Bond, you reappear with the same fatality as the unwanted season." Impossible to get rid of the British agent! The same desire to put an end to the one who keeps coming back to the Afghan prince Kamal Khan, who wants Bond dead once and for all: "Mr. Bond is a rare species that will soon be completely extinct. But the evil international art dealer does not yet know that, for Bond, disappearing means reappearing sooner or later.

Bond continually plays with death, through the staging of his disappearance or games that simulate his death. This is what we might call "a death-reflection". It is as if 007 were split into two: there is the living Bond and the Bond whom everyone believes to be dead, including himself at times. But it is not he who dies, it is his reflection.

Thus, at first glance, 007 has all the appearances of a superhero and the characteristics of a special, vulnerable or invincible being. Bond is a virtuoso of the sensitive, an operator of the reenchantment of reality. Of course, like any agent returning from a mission, Bond is regularly injured: convalescing in a clinic in the Shrublands in *Operation Thunder*; his arm is in a sling in *The World Is Not Enough*, as Bond dislocates his shoulder following an injury caused by a fall from a hot-air balloon; or, in *Skyfall*, he is obliged to retake combat aptitude tests, which he fails, with M hiding this failure from him But the plasticity of the hero is more complex. His shell is reformed and rebuilt. Finally, half-living, half-dead, the body of 007 appears spectral, almost posthuman or superhuman. If the physical body of the British agent is worn and tired by dint of extraordinary missions, we witness its plastic and material recomposition: Bond's body regenerates, comes back and returns. 007 is a spectre. This is the fourth secret, the rebirth or resurrection of the hero. What then can a spectral phenomenology, which concerns ghostly beings, mean? If 007's body is the place of all the pains and sufferings, let us also remember that the carnal envelope is the receptacle or the habitacle of the existence. With Bond as a spectral being, there is no longer any self or unity of subject. Immersed in a violent and destructive world, the secret agent's consciousness perceives the universe as a fragmented whole, made up of lines of force, intensities and asperities. An empty body with scattered affects, the British hero crosses an abrupt and horrifying world. Through his adventures, he makes an essential discovery: James Bond experiences the contingency of human passions. And if the philosopher Jean-Paul Sartre writes that "man is the being through whom nothingness comes into the world", this explanation is even truer if he is a secret agent.

5. PULP STYLE AND POP INTENSITY

> "You are a kite
> dancing in a hurricane."
> Mr. White at 007
> *Spectrum*

Within hours of each other, on the same day, October 5, 1962, two major artistic events were to change world culture forever. One on LP, the other on the big screen, two phenomena with the same initial, the two "B "s, would change pop culture forever. More than a coincidence, it was the simultaneous double birth of James Bond and the Beatles. One in the cinema, *James Bond vs. Doctor No*, the other on record, *Love me do*, the first Beatles single that early fans in Liverpool had been waiting for impatiently for several years. With the two Bs, Bond and Beatles together, the pop culture revolution is underway. But if James Bond is an undeniable symbol of contemporary culture, what are the cultural references mobilized in the films? In other words, does James Bond call upon our classical knowledge or does he put forward more recent and contemporary creations? In the form of simple allusive winks, or with the help of more marked and present references on the screen, 007's films contain numerous cultural indications, as much from the ancient and classical as from the modern and contemporary.

Pulp fiction

The visual saga of James Bond, inspired by Ian Fleming's novels, virtuously re-enacts the confrontation between the Classics and the Moderns, reinvents pop philosophy and thwarts the binary distinction between, on the one hand, the work of art, oriented towards an elitist and demanding creation, the "cinéma d'auteur", and, on the other hand, popular cinema, belonging to the *mainstream* culture and open to a wider public, the "commercial cinema".

What are the references deployed in the 007 saga? What are the winks to current events or to other creations present in the James Bond films? Behind the pure popular entertainment, there are many allusions to ancient and modern times, which open the universe of the British spy to different worlds. The taste for cultural collage, the construction of cinematographic ready-made, are part of 007's narrative arsenal. "Like Andy Warhol, the founding artist of pop art, who had a series of plywood replicas of supermarket boxes made for his Factory in Manhattan, at 213 East 47th Street, including the famous *Brillo Box*, James Bond uses elements of popular culture, whose use he diverts, to insert them into the action and espionage. Besides, doesn't p.o.p. mean *personal opinion on pop*? The diverted use, to interpret personally and in another way, is a process of transformation or attribution of a new identity. By playing on the referents of the mass culture, the cinema of James Bond reinvents the post-industrial universe.

Behind the blockbuster device, many aesthetic elements - sound, image, color, speed and rhythm - invite us to take another look at the world around us. Hijacking classical codes while playing with modern references, 007's films go beyond the quarrel between the past and the contemporary, sublimate the opposition between the ancient and the postmodern and reverse the debate between tradition and renewal.

There is no simplistic binary vision with James Bond. On the contrary, through an original mix of genres and references, the adventures of 007 bring into play the reinvention of new socio-cultural identities. Such is the revelation of the fifth and final secret of James Bond.

The remains of the day

The 007 style is unique. From a certain point of view, it corresponds to a conventional classicism of which it preserves the old-fashioned and quirky charm. James Bond's personality is neither avant-garde nor revolutionary. Would he then be rather conservative, marking his rejection of ruptures and his refusal of upheavals? Are there only cultural references here in the service of a resolutely traditional work?

In *Goldfinger*, in order not to be disturbed, James Bond cuts the news bulletin that is playing on the radio and that announces the satisfaction of the President on a historical event of which no details are given to the spectator. But the main thing is elsewhere: 007 is with Jill Masterson in her hotel suite. They are about to have dinner together. Sensitive to the gustatory conventions and codes of refined tasting, 007 realizes that the champagne that accompanies them is not cold but lukewarm, which constitutes, according to him, "an outrage to morals". To remedy this, he opens another bottle and goes to the kitchen to look for the precious beverage at the right temperature in the refrigerator. Out loud, he declares what can be considered 007's first aesthetic and cultural manifesto: "You can't drink a warm Dom Pérignon any more than you can listen to the Beatles without earplugs. Would this capital declaration register 007 resolutely on the side of the Classics ?

If James Bond is not particularly fond of the Beatles in the 1964 vintage, he is no more fond of the crooner style of American song in the 2015 vintage. In *Spectre*, while borrowing the car reserved for 009 from Q, Bond presses the "Atmosphere" button in the vehicle's special options. The words "Music enabled for 009" appear and the song *New York, New York*, in the 1979 version by Frank Sinatra, echoes in the car's cabin, where 007 cries out, "Oh, no!" before ejecting himself from the car, not really for a musical reason, but to escape the tough and silent Mr. Hinx.

It is true that James Bond's culture is more classical than contemporary. He is able, for example in *Spectre, to* quote a Latin reference in one of his worst moments, while being tortured by Blofeld, in the latter's base in the heart of the Sahara. Tied up on a torture chair, remotely manipulated by the Spectre's leader, the British agent slips into Madeleine Swann's ear the expression *Tempus fugit.* This quotation comes from Book III of the *Georgics* by the Roman poet Virgil, verse 284, and is a perfect example of our hero's classical culture.

In the same way, on the side of the song, to the variety or the pop music, 007, more elitist, prefers the opera. Thus, confusing pleasure and mission, he went to the Academy of Fine Arts in Bratislava, Slovakia, to listen to *String Quartet No. 2 in D major*, composed by Alexander Borodin, famous for its third slow *notturno* movement, performed by the cellist Kara Milovy, whom Bond was soon to meet. A major sign of the excellence of the signature, the musician never separates herself from the Lady Rose, an instrument made by the Italian luthier Stradivarius of Cremona in 1724.

One also remembers that Bond has classic references for wines and champagnes. This is also true for cigars. When he arrives in Cuba, in *Die Another Day*, he goes to a factory in Havana and asks the manager for special cigars, *delectados*. The manager replies, "We haven't made them for thirty years. Bond justifies his choice, showing that he knows the steps involved in making Havana, as well as the three types of leaf needed to make Cuban tobacco, *volado*, *seco* and *ligero*. It is true that this is more a culture of luxury, rather than a classic culture.

Another trait of conventional Anglo-Saxon knowledge that the secret agent possesses is his knowledge of ornithology and entomology. This is obviously a nod to the origin of his name, "James Bond", chosen by Ian Fleming in reference to one of the books he had in the library of his estate, GoldenEye, in Jamaica: *A field guide to the birds of the West Indies* (1936). Its author was none other than James Bond, an American scientist and ornithology curator, born in Philadelphia in 1900 and died in 1989, a butterfly enthusiast and an expert on the wildlife of the Caribbean.

In *Her Majesty's Secret Service*, the spy goes to the estate of M, who owns a small Regency-style mansion in Quaterdeck, near Windsor Castle. As he enters this country estate, Admiral M is working on his lepidopteran collection, and our Commander comments: "Very small, this *Nymphalis polychloris*!" M marks a time of surprise: "007, do you know anything about lepidopterans?" Homage to the origin: the British agent shares the knowledge of his American namesake.

The old reference book is everywhere: in *Octopussy*, when Bond leafs through *A field guide to the birds of the West Indies*. But also in *Die Another Day*, when, in Havana, in the office of Raoul, the director of the cigar factory he has already met, and while he is asking about the gene therapy clinic on the island of Los Organos, 007 takes in hand the totem book on the shelf of the sleeping agent.

The underwater fauna is not in rest. Pretending to be an oceanographer named Robert Sterling, 007 immediately identifies the rare fish *Pterois volitans*. The other species of fish avoid it. Its dorsal spines are loaded with venom. "Majestic, but deadly", he explains to Karl Stromberg, who, suspicious, questions him, thus proving, with flying colors, his knowledge of marine animals.

In addition, there are many literary references throughout the saga: Dante Alighieri, the Florentine poet; Lawrence, the British writer and officer, supporter of Middle Eastern independence; Ernest Hemingway, the novelist and travel journalist; and Tennyson, the most famous British poet of the Victorian period.

When, at the top of the Piz Gloria mountain, in *Her Majesty's Secret Service*, Bond visits the Bleuchamp Institute - the research center for allergies created by Blofeld (hay fever, seafood, chicken and poultry...) where the Spectre is preparing a bacteriological war based on the Omega virus - he ends up going to the basement of the fortress to access the scientific laboratory. The setting then changes. The film, suddenly dark and cold, takes us into the darkness. There is no doubt in our minds: Blofeld's underground lair recreates the entrance to the underworld in *The Divine Comedy*!

It is also that spies, adventurers and adventurers greet each other: Thomas Edward Lawrence, the master of the desert, comes to mind when, wearing the traditional dress of the Bedouins of the desert, Bond crosses the Egyptian Sahara to visit his old Cambridge classmate, Sheik Hosein. In this silent crossing, on the back of a dromedary, is Bond not the perfect reincarnation of Lawrence of Arabia?

Another cultural trait: summoned by his superior in *Licence to Kill,* Bond has an appointment in a highly literary place, Ernest Hemingway's house, in Key West, Florida, where the American writer lived from 1927 to 1939. Upon arriving at the *Hemingway House*, 007 tells his superior his desire to retire, quoting the title of one of the novelist's masterpieces, written precisely on his property in 1929, *A Farewell to Arms.*

A final literary reference - it would be impossible to list them all - is offered in *Skyfall*, when M appears before the Defense and Security Committee to account for the "00" program and the disappearance of a diskette containing the list of NATO secret agents infiltrated into terrorist organizations. To emphasize that while the world has changed, the classic values of espionage have not disappeared, M quotes Alfred Tennyson calmly and solemnly: "If we are not today that force which once moved heaven and earth, we are what we are. Heroic hearts of one kind, weakened by time and fate, but strong by the will to struggle, to explore, to discover, and not to yield." These lines by Tennyson come from the third stanza of his poem *Odysseus,* written in 1833.

As these grave words are spoken, 007, out on the street, is running at full speed from the station exit to the courtroom. With this mad dash, he tries to get there in time and prevent Silva from entering to murder M. He may be old, he may be worn out by years and work, but Bond, in perfect resonance with Tennyson, is still the most effective bulwark against the violence of the world.

All around the world

Beyond the European culture, the cultures of the world are highlighted in the saga. James Bond travels around the planet and, during his missions, makes us discover other thoughts, other spaces, other experiences or sensations. The adventures of 007 are thus part of a multicultural opening.

When he arrives in Japan in *You Only Live Twice,* the British agent attends an official fight of traditional wrestlers. But before that, he goes through a sumo school, called a stable *heya,* where the students are seen training. The class is given by an *oyakata,* a stable master. Then, in an overheated audi-torium, Bond takes his place to attend the fight, in this case a traditional tournament. Part dance, part sport, part martial art and part physical combat, sumo is a fight in which two wrestlers compete according to very strict rules, with ancient religious origins. This characteristic ritual is performed before each engagement, the *shintō*, dedicated to the gods. On a circular-shaped confrontation area called a *dohyō*, wrestlers come to the fight dressed in a *mawashi*, a strip of cloth that surrounds the waist and crotch. James Bond attends, in the audience, the sacred prayer before and after the duel between the opponents. In this scene from *On ne vit que deux fois*, the camera highlights the splendor of the referee's clothing, *gyōji*, the technique of the headdresses, *tokoyama*, the unique chanting of the spectators and supporters, urged on by the fight announcers, *yobidashi*, and the incredible atmosphere of the audience, which participates in the spectacle.

In *Diamonds Are Forever*, the viewer is given a guided tour of Amsterdam: before the scene focuses on the grisly discovery, the body of Miss Whistler pulled from the canal by the Dutch police, the camera offers a glimpse of the beauties of the Dutch capital. First, the Skinny Bridge, or *Magere Brug*, one of the most famous buildings in the Netherlands. In the center of the city, this white-painted wooden double-drawn bascule bridge, built in 1670, connects the two banks of the Amstel River, between the Keizersgracht and the Prinsengracht. Afterwards, we discover a visual panorama of the houses painted by Rembrandt, one of the greatest baroque painters, who settled in the Dutch capital from 1631.

In *The Man with the Golden Gun*, James Bond visits the garden and mausoleum of a Bangkok businessman in business with Scaramanga, Hai Fat. In his garden one can admire dozens of statues that populate and decorate the green space. In Thailand, these statues, of religious inspiration, represent real fighters, mysterious animals or mythical deities. From the 6th century, the art of *dvaravati* was forged, structuring the creation and the Buddhist cosmogony. The garden presented in the film illustrates *Devaravati* art, notably the figures of *yaksha*, terrifying ancient warriors dressed in gold, enamel and colored glass, who protect the entrance to the temples. Later in the film, James Bond joins Andrea Anders to watch a popular Thai boxing event. This martial art has its historical roots in *muay boran* and *krabi krabong*. In the 16th century, the training of this sport was done in the military context. Today, the match between two athletes on a ring, also called *muay thai*, is a very popular confrontation. By the way, 007 arrives late in the stand: "Sorry for the delay, the traffic in Bangkok is worse than in Piccadilly Circus in London", he says when he finally reaches his seat.

In *The Spy Who Loved Me*, the marvelous history of Ancient Egypt is honored during a sound and light show on the Giza plateau, near Cairo, with live commentary for the audience present on site and also for the film's viewers. In front of the pyramids and the Sphinx, we rediscover the great stages of the construction of the pyramids by the pharaohs and the Egyptians of Antiquity. The voice that explains the splendors illuminated by the show evokes "the Sun God who rises on the banks of the Nile". Then the action takes place inside a room of the dead, in front of the sacred hieroglyphs. We are then in the monumental tomb of the pharaoh Khufu, who reigned under the IVth dynasty, more than 4 500 years ago. In the center of the funeral complex, the pyramid of one hundred and fifty meters high and a base of two hundred and thirty-five meters is the only one of the seven wonders of the ancient world still visible today. The decor of the film is then sumptuous, enchanting and spectacular.

In the same film, we see a confrontation between Bond, Amasova and Jaws, this time in broad daylight, in the middle of the ruins of Luxor, the temple dedicated to the cult of Amun and located in the heart of ancient Thebes. With vanishing lines that cross the cinematographic frame, and breathtaking visual shots. For example, Jaws, 007's largest adversary, is tiny, like a barely visible ant, next to the gigantic columns of the Egyptian temple. Shooting from the sky, the camera overhangs the scene, and the microscopic size of the characters, in the middle of superb mythological scenery, seems to create a moment of solemn eternity. The divine height, through the ancient elements and the distant shots, gives a result that mixes the mystery of the pyramids and the pharaohs with police investigation and espionage. The same effect of solemnity is achieved when Bond's distinguished silhouette enters the catacombs, whose entrance resembles that of the temple of Abu Simbel, dug into the rock. This *hemisphere*, dedicated to the cult of Amun, Ra, Ptah and Ramses II, is currently home to MI6 headquarters.

In the midst of the statues and deities, Miss Eve Moneypenny suddenly appears, like an apparition, an iconic and majestic figure. Like Cleopatra, 007's faithful ally is always a Queen, not of England, but of Egypt this time.

As we can see, there are many historical and cultural references. In *Operation Thunderbolt*, at the request of the Spectre organization, the British government has to strike the clock on Big Ben seven times, instead of six, at precisely 18:00. A BBC news release then tells us a useful and interesting piece of British history: the last time such a seemingly technical failure occurred was in 1898, when a violent storm caused the London clock to go haywire.

In *The Man with the Golden Gun*, Bond comes across the American sheriff J. W. Pepper, who is sightseeing on the canals of Bangkok. Mistakenly handcuffed by the national police, he protests and mentions the name of the American political scientist and diplomat, Secretary of State during the Nixon presidency and winner of the Nobel Peace Prize in 1973: "I'll get Henry Kissinger." A very important name in classical political references.

In *Moonraker*, the cruel Hugo Drax organizes a hunt for pheasant, partridge and duck in his royal gardens, surrounded by counts and countesses. Just as James Bond arrives in a Rolls-Royce in a very classical outfit, Drax's hunting horn sounds the end of the hunt. The musician then plays the first three notes of the introduction to the symphonic poem *Thus Spoke Zarathustra, set to* music and composed by Richard Strauss in

1896. This brief sound extract illustrates the ultra-classicism of the master of the house, Hugo Drax.

In *For Your Eyes Only*, the reference to the Iron Lady who ruled the United Kingdom from 1979 to 1990 is more direct and explicit. The first female Prime Minister telephones 007 to congratulate him on the success of his mission. The telephone conversation does not take place with Bond, but with the parrot Max, who belongs to the Havelock family. Here, humor is used to divert the classic political references of the 20th century.

James Bond also has, on a personal level, a very good historical knowledge: in Tangier, facing Brad Whitaker, fascinated by the great battles of history and by bloodthirsty military generals, 007 gives a lesson to the crook, in *Killing is not playing*, while confronting him in his sophisticated armory. In front of models of the arms dealer's toy soldiers, Agent James Bond corrects his enemy's historical errors and shares his theoretical knowledge of events. Bond knows exactly where the third infantry charge took place, on the last day of the Battle of Gettysburg in 1863: "Pickett charged at Cemetery Ridge, not Little Round Top," says 007.

Other traits of his personality refer to a classical culture. James Bond, as we know, has a very good command of the languages of several countries. And if French is the language of diplomacy in the great courts of Europe in the nineteenth century, it should be remembered that French replaces Latin from the eighteenth century for the drafting and signing of international treaties, with that of Rastatt in 1714. The *lingua franca* was praised by leaders and diplomats for its logical and geometric precision. It is the recognition of the international cultural influence of France. In the James Bond films, the French language has a new function, less political but just as prestigious: French is the language of casino games. It is probably for this reason that 007 expresses himself correctly in French. When he arrives by car at the Monte Carlo casino in *GoldenEye* and the door is opened for him, he says in impeccable French: "Bonsoir Pierre, ça va bien?"

Bond's opponents have the same concern for propriety and distinction, the same ancient culture and respect for the prestigious past. The world of the enemies of freedom and democracy is as delicate as it is refined, as cruel as it is classical: among the most dangerous criminals, Blofeld is a lover of twilight romantic poetry, which he recites with his prisoner. He is also capable, as he prepares to launch nuclear attacks on Russia, China and the United States, of quoting the maxim of a moralist of the Grand Siècle. Karl Stromberg, on the other hand, decorates his amphibious palace with murals reminiscent of Italian Renaissance painting. As for Hugo Drax, he quotes Oscar Wilde and plays the music of Chopin. On the other hand, the terrorist and criminal members of the Quantum organization meet at the opera to prepare the "Tierra" project while listening to Puccini. And finally, in another register, Blofeld is also passionate about meteorites, even if the geological reference to the oldest stone ever held by a human being, the Kartenhoff, is fictitious, its conservation and its presence in Blofeld's desert sanctuary confirm his megalomania and his desire for domination. Among the hero's enemies, another cruel and diabolical adversary, the terrorist Silva, is a music lover, and associates his crimes with extracts of heady music.

The Spectre's leader is able to impress 007 with his culture of quotations. In the final phase of his satellite attack plan, in *Diamonds Are Forever*, when he threatens the civil and military security of many governments around the world, Blofeld quotes a classic 17th century socialite author. The man with the cat remembers an author who frequented the salons, those of Madame de Sablé and Madame de Lafayette, and who specialized in an aesthetic of the short form and a literature of short genre (bills, sentences, reflections, maxims, small speeches). It is a question you guessed it of the rebel François de La Rochefoucauld. His *Maximes*, which denounce self-love, are famous. Blofeld quotes from memory and reproduces an incomplete quote, "Humility is the worst form of vanity." Blofeld's phrasing is not entirely accurate, since the real quote is, "Humility is an artifice of pride that stoops to elevate itself." Even though the dreaded Spectre leader recites a truncated quote, James is still speechless.

With Karl Stromberg, we are also faced with a megalomaniac, cold and bloodthirsty loner. The individual is passionate about the violence and beauty of the ocean floor. Another Captain Nemo, like Doctor No: "The underwater world is so vast and unexplored", says the dangerous and rich Stromberg after having captured the submersibles *Ranger* and *Potemkin*. His lair, the Atlantis, which can descend or rise to the surface, is luxurious. In his gigantic royal lounge, the man who hires the hitman Jaws decorates his portholes with hangings and tapestries. Hanging on the walls to decorate the room, these pictorial elements reproduce classical works in the style of *The Birth of Venus*, a major work of the Italian Renaissance, painted by Botticelli around 1485. If this painting expresses the aerial element - with the breath of the god Zephyr in *contrapposto* - as well as the softness of the spring wind, the marine and maritime elements are also very present in the masterpiece of Italian art: Venus emerges from the waters, standing in the conch of a shell. The waves are slightly agitated, pink flowers and reeds float on the surface of the water, the ocean seems calm and only small waves lightly wash up on the shore. When the tapestries of Karl Stromberg's sumptuous reception room rise, the whole set-up takes on its full majesty. The submarine base seems to rise out of the water and into the sky from the sea, carried by a divine breath. During this ascent from the depths of the sea to the surface, majestic music, imbued with calm and solemnity, accompanies this technical rebirth. Mozart's *piano concerto number 21*, composed in Vienna in 1785, gives the aquatic scene its full power.

The same atmosphere of solemnity and grandiose splendor is present when James Bond enters Hugo Drax's castle, which has been transported stone by stone from France to California. In the living room of his royal residence, Hugo

Drax is at the piano. He is playing Frédéric Chopin's "The Drop of Water", *Prelude Op. 28 No. 15 in D-flat major*. It is one of the twenty-four preludes of the Polish virtuoso pianist, composed during the winter of 1838-1839 when Chopin was vacationing with George Sand on the island of Mallorca, at the Carthusian monastery of Valldemossa. In a lyrical and charming way, the piece reproduces the repetition of raindrops, before moving on to a more sombre and sombre part to imitate thunder and storm.

After this musical interlude, Hugo Drax takes advantage of this classical and traditional climate to quote an Irish author of the nineteenth century or, more exactly, to divert one of his phrases. He pastiche an excerpt from the theatrical comedy about Victorian England, *The Importance of Being Earnest*, a play premiered in 1895 at the Saint James Theater in London by the poet, writer and playwright, Oscar Wilde. If the original quote is "To lose one parent may be regarded as a misfortune, to lose both looks like carelessness", Hugo Drax wonders: "How would Oscar Wilde have presented the situation? To have lost one plane may be bad luck, to lose two becomes carelessness."

In *Quantum of Solace,* several members of the Quantum criminal organization, the future nucleus of the larger Spectre project, meet at the Bregenz Opera House in Austria. While the set is modern, with a giant eye in the middle of the stage, and a strange scaffolding is set up to carry the singers, chorus and soloists up high, the play is classical. It is Giacomo

Puccini's 1900 masterpiece, a love and patriotic drama, *Tosca*. Thanks to an ingenious technological stratagem, as fast as it is effective, Bond manages to unmask some of the members of the group, some of whom immediately flee: Dominic Greene, Gregor Karakov, Moishe Soref, Guy Haines. The Pale King, better known as Mr. White, remains seated to continue enjoying the show. Then, through a virtuoso camerawork, thanks to a rhythmic alternation of images, the fake shootings on stage mix with the real action in the restaurant of the theater. Bond shoots down his pursuers while the show also stages death. Here we witness a cinematic mise en abyme: illusory death on stage, real death hovering over the secret agent. As in medieval heraldry, when the figures of the coat of arms are superimposed on one another. Through the duplication structure of the medallion, the mise en abyme exposes a theory of reciprocity. Art and artifice duplicate each other. By representing death on the stage, while the violent action takes place behind the scenes, in this case in the restaurant of the Bregenz opera house, the mise en abyme sheds light on the creative process. Recall the famous scene ii of Act III of Shakespeare's *Hamlet*, when comedy actors perform a play that represents the murder of the hero's father. Is the violence of espionage just an artifice? Are James Bond films, in fact, nothing more than a lyrical orchestration, a baroque drama, an imaginary opera?

While occupying a deserted island off the coast of Macau, emptied of its inhabitants, cyber-terrorist Silva has had speakers installed throughout the abandoned city. Taking Bond, his hostage, with him for a special execution session, Silva turns on the music in the urban speakers. Suddenly, a song comes on: Charles Trenet's "Boum", released in 1938. The killer Silva seems to enjoy the explosive and destructive resonances of this hijacked love song. "When our heart goes boom," Charles Trenet sings at the top of his lungs, "the whole world goes boom," Silva says with amusement, forcing James Bond, at the same time, to shoot the frightened Séverine.

Back to the future

How do the references in the films define an aesthetic universe? Can we also read in them the ideological signs of a social and cultural marking? When Blofeld and Drax divert quotations from François de La Rochefoucauld and Oscar Wilde, 007's sworn enemies seek to show their hold on art and culture. In their enterprise of manipulation and destruction, they display a sadism and a cruelty, including on the history of arts and on the beauty of works. To divert the art, to subject the culture, perverse and violent way to affirm still more their power and their domination on the society of the men, on the past, the present and the future. Megalomania and perversity mixed.

But does James Bond himself have classical tastes or is he more attracted to the contemporary?

When he meets Q on a bench in the National Gallery in London, in *Skyfall*, 007 is pensive. In front of him is one of the most beautiful paintings by William Turner (1775-1851), a painter, watercolorist and printmaker, a romantic master of light. The painting Bond is looking at is the 1839 *Fighting Temeraire*, a sailing vessel returning to port for the last time, pulled by a steam tug. The great ship of the line belongs to the past of sailing, and the past is gradually fading away, signifying the twilight of an old era, and the dawn of a new one. However, the one who comments most emotionally on the painting is not 007, but Q who has just arrived and sat down next to him. Q confides on his impressions: "It always makes me a little melancholic. The venerable galleon ignominiously scrapped. It's the inevitability of time."

Nor is Bond sensitive, in the same film *Skyfall,* to the painting *Woman with a Fan*, painted by Modigliani in 1919. When he goes to Shanghai, filmed at night and illuminated by the neon and blue lights of the city, 007 follows the killer Patrice who aims at a potential buyer of the painting in the building opposite his own. Between Patrice and 007, there is a sublimely filmed shadow fight in front of a gigantic fluorescent robotic jellyfish. The painting *Woman with a Fan* is one of the five paintings stolen from the Museum of Modern Art in Paris in May 2010. The real and mysterious theft has not yet been solved by the police. The film *James Bond vs. Doctor No* already alluded to a painting that had really disappeared and possibly been stolen by Doctor No - in this film, 007 notices its presence in the island lair, and finds it strange that it should be there. Moreover, in a nod to the first film of the saga, we find the painting *Woman with a Fan* by Modigliani, present in *Skyfall,* and in *Spectre* inside the deserted base of Blofeld in North Africa. The painting hangs on the wall in the room where Madeleine Swann - whose name is an obvious reference to Marcel Proust's *The Search for Lost Time* - is "trapped".

In fact, there are many hints that *Spectre is* a remake of *James Bond vs. Doctor No.* Beyond the stolen paintings in both films, in 1962, James Bond and Honey Rider are holding hands, moments away from meeting the one who is holding them captive, Doctor No. As Honey Rider points out that she has sweaty hands, James Bond to reassure her says, "I'm scared too." In 2015, in the back of the Rolls-Royce that drives them to Blofeld's lair, Madeleine Swann says, "I'm scared James." So 007, to comfort her, takes her hand. In 1962, James Bond tells Doctor No, "Our madhouses are full of Napoleons and Gods." In 2015, James Bond tells Blofeld, "Visionaries, our asylums are full of them." Same madness, same cruelty, same violence. From 1962 to 2015, the Bond universe has not changed, it remains the same. But is Bond, who is not so sensitive to classical art, more sensitive to modern art?

James Bond films not only showcase technical and technological feats, but also contemporary cultural and scientific advances. For example, a long scene in *Casino Royale* takes place at the Miami Science Center, when 007 follows Dimitrios to a famous anatomical exhibition, "Body Worlds,

Our Body," which has been a sensation since its inception. Highlighting the inside of the human body in a virtual, intimate and realistic way, the exhibition takes visitors through the organs, muscles and membranes of the human skeleton with technological prowess, just as Leonardo da Vinci or Andreas Vesalius did in their medical work. Simply, the techniques and special effects put in place by the anatomist Gunther von Hagens, thanks to an innovative performance of conservation of the bodies, allow to see differently the fine structures of the human being. One of the most famous reconstructions in this exhibition, which has been shown around the world several times, is called "Poker Playing Trio". This work of art or anatomical installation, depending on the point of view, represents three flayed bodies playing cards around a casino table. It plays an important role in the plot of *Casino Royale*, as Dimitrios places the S3 pass on top of a pile of gambling chips, allowing James Bond to retrieve his bag from the locker room.

Bond is a man of his time who enjoys the benefits of the modern age. Like everyone else, he likes to relax and enjoy the entertainment of the society in which he lives. Relaxed during his missions, Bond often takes the opportunity to have a good time. We don't know exactly which novels he enjoys and reads in his spare time, except of course for his "own" one, the bird book, but he may also flip through a "popular" magazine or newspaper during his mission. In Bern, in *Her Majesty's Secret Service*, Bond sneaks into the office of the lawyer Gebrüder

Gumbold to obtain secret information about Count Balthazar de Bleuchamp. After sending a heavy safe-lock decryption machine through the window, 007 takes advantage of the lawyer's lunch break to search the room in his office for top-secret documents. But, while the machine identifies codes and numbers, 007 settles in an armchair to read the *Playboy* newspaper. While the lawyer, not suspecting anything, goes up in the elevator and is about to return to the door of his office, 007 comes out urgently, taking with him the central poster of the famous magazine for men.

Apart from his interest in light reading of *Playboy*, what are 007's other postmodern references? *In The Man with the Golden Gun*, during a prodigious stunt to reach the other side of a river by jumping over a barge, Bond mentions a recent popular figure. He is a famous American stuntman and motorcyclist. As the car accelerates and gains momentum to cross the river, 007 indeed turns to his passenger, as if to warn him of what he is about to attempt and what might happen: "You know Evel Knievel?"

More widely, there are many pop references in the 007 films. The spirit of the popular culture crosses the films of the James Bond saga: we find the *Nautilus* of Jules Verne, the compressed sculpture of the artist César, the films with suspense of Alfred Hitchcock, Steven Spielberg, Sergio Leone, Georges Lucas, Michael Curtiz, Stanley Kubrick or Orson Welles.

Some of the British agent's enemies are more oriented towards a fantastic universe and a pop imagination. Thus

Doctor No built his sanctuary on a mysterious island, and his impressive underwater lounge is worthy of resembling the *Nautilus*. Architect of his own fortress, he drew the plans himself: this universe with a retro-futuristic aesthetic, both eerie and fabulous, plunges us into the bowels of the sea. The glass of the aquarium, convex ice of 25 mm, makes magnifying glass and shows the fascination of Doctor No for the underwater world, as in *Twenty thousand leagues under the sea*, the novel of Jules Verne published in 1869.

In *Goldfinger*, the vehicle of the gangster Mr. Solo is compacted in the Atlantic Iron Metal company. What is left of his car, reduced to a box of scrap metal and metal, looks like a pop work by César Baldaccini, known as "César", a French sculptor and member of the New Realists, an artistic movement born in the 1960s, and a specialist in the compression technique.

In *Her Majesty's Secret Service*, 007 is unmasked by Blofeld: "The de Bleuchamp's are not buried in a cathedral, but in a church, Saint Anne's. Sir Hilary would have known that. A slight 007 faux pas, you don't become a heraldist." Following this discovery of his identity, Bond finds himself locked in a dark room, a space made of cogs. This infernal, nightmarish machine, an aestheticization of mental torture, immediately evokes the psychoanalytical settings created by the painter Salvador Dali in Alfred Hitchcock's 1945 film *Spellbound*. The following scene, which mixes endless stairs, pulleys, electric cables, scaffolding and winches of a cable car, evokes other

Hitchcock's films: not this time an interior universe, mental and dreamlike of a dream, but an exterior space that the human being, tiny in front of this immensity, must climb or conquer, like the monument of Mount Rushmore, of South Dakota, in *North by Northwest* of the famous director.

In *Moonraker*, James Bond discovers a clandestine laboratory in Venice. The melody he has to reproduce by ear on the secret digicode of the laboratory is the one used in the sequence of the contact with the extraterrestrial ships in the film *Encounters of the Third Kind* directed by Steven Spielberg in 1977, the same year in which *Star Wars IV, A New Hope* by George Lucas was released, two essential references of *Moonraker*, released in theaters two years later. This very famous melody, composed of only five notes (*B* flat, *C*, *A* flat, *A* flat and *E* flat, with an octave change on the second and fourth notes) was created on an ARP 2500 synthesizer. This short ritornello was invented by a composer of many film scores, John Williams.

Also in *Moonraker*, when Bond sends Chang through the clock face of the Torre dell'Orologio, in Venice, Hugo Drax's faithful killer ends up crushed on a concert piano, in the middle of a recital. The classical opera singer stops when Bond says "Play it again, Sam!", referring to the piece of music *As time goes by*, created in 1931 on Broadway, which the character played by Ingrid Bergman, pronouncing this sentence in the film *Casablanca* by Michael Curtiz, in 1942, opposite Humphrey Bogart, wishes to listen to again.

Another film soundtrack in *Moonraker*, a veritable treasure trove of pop culture references: in the South American pampas, Bond is wearing a large cowboy poncho. Accompanied by two other riders, 007 crosses wide open spaces. He rides his horse before going to an old Franciscan monastery, where the men of MI6 train between martial arts and laser shooting. The silhouette of Bond on horseback is reminiscent of Clint Eastwood in the "spaghetti western", popularized by the actor in Sergio Leone's films, notably through the *Dollar Trilogy*, three westerns in 1964, 1965 and 1966.

A new cult reference in the James Bond pop universe: when Hugo Drax's space base, orbiting the earth and undetectable by radar, appears on the screen, the immense city in space is shown in all its splendor and solemnity. Thanks to visual effects, the camera gives an image of the beauty of the interstellar void, evoking the dance of the rockets, the movement of the satellites and the displacement of the planets in *2001, The Space Odyssey, the* epic and ultimate science fiction film. A metaphysical ballet and lunar choreography, the interstellar journey created by Stanley Kubrick offers a unique vision, both sublime and disturbing.

In *Tomorrow Never Dies*, another pop reference is cited, this time by the press, media destabilization and *fake news* magnate, Elliot Carver. Ready for all manipulations and disinformation to dominate the digital communication networks, the *networks* and the GAFA, he uses the power of satellites. He wants to trigger a world crisis by controlling telecommunications and dominating the media. Elliot Carver wants to take as a model William Randolph Hearst , the one who inspired Orson Welles to create his epic, eccentric and megalomaniacal character in *Citizen Kane*: "Great men manipulate the media," says Elliot Carver, "look at William Randolph Hearst who said to the photographers: "Take the pictures, I'll take the war."

Finally, in the modern musical realm, we can mention the role of the vocal and melodic group The Beach Boys. While Bond recovers a microchip hidden in a medallion from 003's corpse in *Dangerously Yours*, a Russian helicopter and armed skiers chase him in Siberia. Pursued, 007 loses first one of his skis, then takes a snowmobile. This last one explodes following a helicopter shooting. The British agent then improvises a snowboard with the rest of the device and goes down the snowy track. At that very moment, the group's 1965 pop hit, *California Girls,* resounds.

In *Killing is Not Playing*, Moneypenny invites James Bond to spend the evening at her house, to enjoy together the music of the crooner and pop singer who performed the hit *Copacabana*: "Come listen to my Barry Manilow records." In the same film, Necros, the KGB killer in the pay of arms dealer Brad Whitaker and General Georgi Koskov, never separates from his Walkman player. He uses it as a weapon to eliminate his adversaries and signs his corpses with the insignia "Smiert Spionom", named after an old Stalin operation, but Necros listens to the same song over and over again, composed by the

Anglo-Saxon rock band The Predenters, formed in 1978. This title belongs to the pop music, it is *Where has everyone gone?* which appears on the studio album *Get close* of 1986.

In *GoldenEye*, 007 allows himself a remark on the vocal qualities of Irina, the fiancée of the Russian mafia boss Valentin Zukovsky: "Does anyone strangle a cat?" This remark leads to the interruption of the rehearsal, on the stage of the nightclub, of the singer then pushing the ditty on the notes of the famous country music title *Stand by your man* by Tammy Wynette. In *Die Another Day*, Bond takes a plane and arrives in London on a British Airways flight. At the same time, a tune plays on the screen, the pop rock hit by ex-punk band The Clash, Joe Strummer's 1980 song *London Calling*.

Finally, to finish this overview of the pulp spirit, personalities from the world of pop culture make cameos or quick appearances in the James Bond saga. Sometimes they slip in for a moment on the screen, furtively and surreptitiously. Dancer, singer and musician Sammy Davis Jr., a member of the Rat Pack, makes a brief appearance in *Diamonds Are Forever*: at the casino of eccentric billionaire Willard Whyte in Las Vegas, Bond quickly runs into him at the craps table. In *Casino Royale*, James Bond quickly runs into one of the most prominent figures in pop culture again, with his hands in the air at a customs checkpoint at Miami airport. It is the inventor of Virgin Cola and the CEO of Virgin Atlantic, the Londoner Richard Branson. Finally, the most famous nod to global pop culture is the role of the fencing coach and teacher, Verity, given to the actress, singer, dancer and glamorous *pop star*, pioneer long before Lady Gaga or Justin Bieber, the artist Madonna.

From Chopin to Madonna, from Virgil to *Playboy*, from Tennyson to Hemingway, the many cultural references in the James Bond saga touch on all genres and styles, in a spirit that goes beyond the opposition of scholarly and popular culture. This is the fifth and final secret of Agent 007's adventures: in the same whirlwind, with the same momentum, the Bond films take on both classic and recent works. This is an innovative flexibility and mobility, which deterritorializes the references, out of their original base. This effect of renewal is also found in the diversity of music chosen to open the films of the saga: Shirley Bassey, Tom Jones, Nancy Sinatra, Louis Armstrong, Paul McCartney and the Wings, Duran Duran, Tina Turner, Madonna, Sheryl Crow, Chris Cornell, Jack White, Alicia Keys, Adele, Sam Smith or Billie Eilish. A dazzling diversity of artists; an ever-renewed singularity of unique creations.

Conclusion.
The latest James Bond films

"Total control has its appeal:
we're watching everyone."
C to M.
Spectrum

With a renewed cinematographic analysis of the twenty-five films of the James Bond saga, from 1962 to 2020, the philoscopic eye, this new method of viewing, has attempted to bring an innovative look at the cinema and the screen.

This singular approach, allowing us to rediscover in a different way the famous adventures of the spy in the service of Her Majesty, was also the occasion to reveal five original secrets, hidden or masked in the visual work. Five thematic and philosophical dilemmas are at the heart of the 007 saga:

politics (cold war or fight against terrorism), identity (British citizenship *versus* globalization of the subject), love (passion of hedonism versus sublimation of romanticism), the body (phenomenology of the real body or ontology of the spectral body) and culture (classical references *versus* pop preferences). These philosophical tracks also allow to open a reflection on aesthetics, art and creation, through the new notion of chaos-cinema.

The five stages of this analysis also wanted to deploy an original and innovative way to give an even greater place, in philosophical studies, to mainstream and popular cinema. In order to achieve this, it was necessary to construct and conceptualize new reading criteria, open to adventure, suspense and espionage.

At the heart of this device: the image-action. It is the only way to associate the text with the screen, the dialogues with the events, the show with the thought.

From *James Bond vs. Doctor No* to *Mourir peut attendre*, the twenty-five films renew spy cinema, with the aesthetic figure of a hero of pure spectacle participating in the codification of popular cinema. But to bring a new deciphering of the action-image, only a rigorous and detailed approach of the scenes allows to apprehend and understand what is played on the screen. Visual choreography, graphic nervousness, jerky editing and rhythmic virtuosity are the four elements used for a new thought of filmic deployment.

However, at the end of this inquiry and investigation, a final question arises, in another register and on a different level. In the face of international events that baffle us by their complexity, and in the face of the world's current events, whose singularity we apprehend every day, where are the authentic James Bond characters? Which personality could *really* embody it? Are there individuals who, in their own way, would carry his heroic, civic and committed values? Do the 007s of our time exist? Perhaps we have found them.

The last action hero

First of all, there is one that, perhaps, without special effects or luxury cars, would correspond to 007's mission in a complex and disturbed international political situation.

To find it, you have to look closely at the 2015 film *Spectre*. *It* becomes clear how much of the enemy comes from within: codenamed "C," Max Denbigh is the head of intelligence in London's new Vauxhall building and director general of the UK's Centre for National Security. While he has merged MI5 with MI6, his political ambition is to build a vast network of global surveillance programs, legally, at the expense of national security services. To achieve absolute control of the flow of digital data, with a view to a globalized union of planetary information, C has set up a committee of which he is the director, the "Nine Sentinels" group, which he presents at a summit organized in the presence of M in Tokyo. Denbigh plans to gain unlimited access to the intelligence of the nine member countries by obtaining a full cooperation agreement from them. The risk of "democratization" threatens the future of citizens and society as a whole. Who could prevent this dangerous project for democracy and individual freedoms? Two men in fact, one, fictional, in *Spectre*; the other, authentic, in reality. Isn't there a common point, here, between the imagination of a work and the truth of the world? In a word, isn't whistleblower Edward Snowden, in the end, our latest James Bond? Even if transparency at all costs is dangerous for democracy, and the balance between revealing confidential information and holding illegitimate data remains to be found, the question is worth asking.

In the face of ultra-technical mass surveillance - implemented in the film by C, which is, in reality, in the service of the Spectre organization - data protection is the main concern of many citizens around the world. Whistleblowers, investigative journalists or *whistleblowers* ("those who blow the whistle", a legal term since 1863), NGOs or members of parliament, unions or citizens are mobilizing and playing this democratic role. In a context of international political crisis, the individual often acts alone, in the face of powerful organizations with considerable means for their action. Fiction and reality come together.

Today, with blogs, videos, photos, conversations, *likes*, *tweets* and other private or professional exchanges, all our lives are recorded, communicated and processed by algorithms. Our society has become a world of surveillance and information. Human experience is transformed into digital data; citizens' lives are captured by machines serving private interests and anti-democratic domination.

Isn't the James Bond saga about monitoring individuals and controlling their every move? If electronic RFID (Radio Frequency Identification) chips are already integrated, in the form of magnetic barcodes, in passports, transport cards or bank cards, the films show the next step, which goes even further in the implementation of tracers. In the 007 films made after the trauma of the World Trade Center attacks and the implementation of the *USA Patriot Act* legislation adopted on October 25, 2001, the panoptic devices of surveillance techniques were reinforced. Thus, from *Casino Royale* onwards, in 2006, a biometric tracking implant is implanted in James Bond's wrist. This large wave transmitter and DGPS (*Differential Global Positioning System*) twenty-four channel receiver transmits the location coordinates to a sonic resonance unit. Traced, monitored and identified at all times, 007 is paradoxically endangered by this excessive surveillance that is supposed to protect him. What M understood perfectly in *Spectre*, in 2015. Thanks to this system called *Smart Blood* in the film, Q, M and Moneypenny can trace, from London, the movements of Bond and Swann in North Africa. Unfortunately, this protection becomes a threat since C also records all of 007's movements. In order to protect their friend, M asks Q and Moneypenny to erase everything: "Bond has to do it himself. Only solution, indeed, to protect him from the tracer. This desire of the modern State to monitor every individual gesture, with a view to disciplining bodies and minds, was already denounced by Michel Foucault in 1975, with his reference to the project of prison observation imagined by Jeremy Bentham in *Panopticon* in 1798.

The secret alliance of the "Five Eyes

If 007 is an agent of secrecy, the whistleblower is the defender of individual privacy, a counterpoint to control and manipulation. The *Panama Papers* revelations, the UBS investigations, the HSBC investigations or the *Luxleaks* and *Swissleaks* scandals remind us that the protection of citizens and the vigilance of populations are essential to the proper functioning of contemporary society. Discovering that our computers and laptops are controlled and monitored without our knowledge, and then denouncing this attack on our individual liberties, these two actions constitute a courageous double step of political counter-power. The awareness that technological mediations and communication networks are only simulacra which harm the confidentiality and the private life of the citizens becomes at once a democratic awakening.

Concerned about the common good and concerned about the collective interest, those who sound the alarm demonstrate democratic freedom, a critical eye, and a desire for justice and equity: media pluralism, citizen experimentation, and a balance of power are counterpowers that must be defended today. Faced with economic control and digital domination, the political courage to oppose the system is often a solitary and isolated approach.

If James Bond is British, Britain is precisely the first country in Europe to adopt a legal arsenal to protect individuals and whistleblowers, thanks to the *Protect* program, which was responsible for the British Parliament passing the *Public Interest Disclosure Act* in 1998. Procedural assistance and legislative guidance are essential to help the *millennial* generation participate in action against digital control platforms in the age of GAFAM (Google, Apple, Facebook, Amazon and Microsoft), BATX (Baidu, Alibaba, Tencent and Xiaomi) and NATU (Netflix, Airbnb, Tesla and Uber).

If electronic technology and the generalized connectivity of *Big Data* impact our environment, our mentalities, our behaviors and societal evolutions, how can we avoid the drifts? Among the most terrible adversaries of James Bond, in the recent 007 movies, we find cybercriminals who use digital hyperconnectivity as a weapon to destabilize the economy, culture and politics: In *GoldenEye* the computer programmer Boris Grishenko of the Severnaya Space Weapons Control Center in Siberia, in *Tomorrow Never Dies* the powerful tycoon Elliot Carver of the Carver Media Group (CMG), in *Skyfall* the cybercriminal and computer hacker Silva, a former field agent in Hong Kong who wants revenge, or, in *Spectre*, Ernst Stavro Blodeld who sets up a huge technological data processing network from a *data center* installed in the middle of the Sahara desert in which hundreds of *data analysts* and system designers work for him. The head of the criminal organization uses all the real and possible operations of the virtual network, manipulating the sequencing speeds and processing capacities, to organize a vast data network, a deployment of control and surveillance of information capable of initiating a process of destruction of countries, threatening governments and generalized chaos of democracies. At the secret meeting of the Spectre organization in Rome, in the Palazzo Cardenza, Blofeld mentions the terrorist attacks in Hamburg, Tunisia, Mexico City, before the one planned for South Africa.

Moreover, if the enemy also comes from within in the James Bond films with the character of C - coordinator of the British security services and traitor in Blofeld's pay, he transmits information from the member countries of the Nine Sentinels to the criminal organization - it is the same in reality. Edward Snowden, a twenty-nine year old computer scientist, discovered a gigantic surveillance program, involving tens of thousands of telephone calls and online exchanges, set up by the United States and Great Britain.

Two Anglo-Saxon state agencies - the U.S. government's electronic intelligence agency, the National Security Agency (NSA), and the U.K.'s Government Communications Headquarters (GCHQ) - have engaged in massive, illegal and shocking electronic espionage that violates the protection and privacy of communications. The young expert analyst, working for an NSA subcontractor, brought out documents from the offices of the U.S. Cryptologic Center revealing the activities of these most powerful electronic surveillance agencies on the planet.

Snowden showed that these agencies had privileged access to the servers of the digital giants: Facebook, Google, Yahoo, YouTube, Skype, Apple or Microsoft. The NSA collects two hundred million messages per day worldwide. This system, which also carries out more targeted eavesdropping, from Angela Merkel to the European Commission, from the Swift financial network to NGOs such as Doctors of the World, is at the service of a clandestine cooperation, the alliance of the so-called *Fives Eyes:* the illegality of encryption and decryption serves the interests of the five countries that are the United States, Great Britain, Canada, Australia and New Zealand. If opening a website or sending an email is a simple operation, practiced every day by millions of users, Snowden's revelations have shown the absolute necessity of a debate on the neutrality of networks and the defense of citizens' rights in the digital age. And this, in order to release the guarantees of a right and a legislation for the future, the only conditions for a fundamental digital freedom.

How to protect the flow of data on the Web? Only a specialist, an expert in digital networks, is able to measure the current state of digital culture. Only he can combine and follow five joint perspectives, the technical conditions, the historical evolution, the legal bases, the social links and the political implications, in order to identify the guarantees of a fundamental digital right and freedom.

ED, the spy who loves us ?

From the spy to the whistleblower, there is only one step and many common points bring 007 and Snowden together. So what is the parallel between JB and ES?

One day in May 2013, the patriot and defender of freedoms Edward Snowden left Honolulu on the island of Hawaii for Hong Kong: under the pseudonym of spy *Verax* ("Truth" in Latin) he gave an appointment at a top-secret location to three journalists, Laura Poitras, Ewen MacAskill and Glenn Greenwald, of the British daily *The Guardian*. In his secret agent's briefcase, four computers and 50,000 highly confidential files from the NSA and GCHQ on several USB keys. *Verax* makes public and provides the world with the truth about an international system of surveillance of electronic and telephone metadata of millions of citizens, set up by the *Fives Eyes*, thanks to undersea fiber optic cables through which global communications transit.

Moreover, before becoming the clandestine *Verax* whistleblower, Edward Snowden, a gifted computer scientist and network engineer, was a secret agent. "Before I worked for the government, but today I serve everyone," he declares at the opening of his memoirs: at 25, a CIA agent assigned to the American embassy in Switzerland, he lives under diplomatic cover in Geneva in a luxurious apartment overlooking Lake Geneva; at 26, Snowden leaves for Japan, under a false identity, in order to set up a secret network for the NSA, just as James Bond himself goes to Japan under an assumed name. On the one hand, in reality, Edward Snowden is officially hired as a service provider and employed by the company Dell, while he is a real spy and computer scientist for the NSA. In Japan, under his cover, he develops *EpicShelter, an* epic data backup system. On the other hand, in fiction, James Bond goes to Tokyo to investigate the Osato company. To do this, he takes the alias of Fisher, an industrial engineer from Empire Chemicals. Bond and Snowden, the two men have a false identity to carry out their Asian mission.

But while they are both patriots and Anglo-Saxon citizens, Bond and Snowden know how to confront society with itself and force it to question its laws, its organization, its values. Snowden makes sedition and disobeys. He flees and goes into exile. Bond is a dissident agent who emancipates himself, watched by his superiors, ready to resign on numerous occasions. In different ways, they both assert their freedom, their desire for emancipation and their individual conscience.

To no longer trust blindly the laws of one's country, to bring a critical eye to the functioning of the judiciary and to have a citizen's vigilance on the national institutions, this step is a committed ethical choice. It is simply called becoming a political subject. In their own way, Bond and Snowden offer us two attitudes of loyalty to democracy and commitment to the service of the community. They pick up the gauntlet, accept the challenge and throw themselves into the fight for freedom. We can salute them for this, even if radical transparency also involves dangers and abuses. Indeed, Edward Snowden himself concludes, in his memoirs, regarding the link between the spy and the whistleblower, as well as the notion of privacy: "The most transparent democracy in the world must be able to refuse to disclose the identity of its secret agents." As a response to the initial plot of *Skyfall*, where the threat of disclosure on the web of undercover secret agents looms, it is a matter of keeping our eyes open and confronting ourselves, over and over again, with our own responsibility to democratic society.

From Pussy Galore to Pussy Riot

In the James Bond films, the spy, or the spywoman, regularly changes narrative and fictional identity. Making his or her likeness "blurred" is a classic operative gesture: becoming a multiple being makes it possible to blur his or her subjective unity and to make it uncertain in the eyes of others. Becoming other is part of the activity of the secret agent. The spy is an incarnation of the division of the subject, who is not what he seems to be and can individualize himself in another way. This is the case when 007, in order to pass incognito to the East, becomes in a few moments Charles Moreton, representative of a manufacturer from Leeds visiting furniture factories in the GDR. The transformation must escape the grip of knowledge. Playing with various figures in order to be elusive, such is the metamorphosis of the secret agent. In order not to be locked into a single identity, it is necessary to blur the tracks and disrupt the genres. In this context, the stylization of the body operates strongly, shifting the modalities of self-construction.

But the identity disorder can also concern the issues of masculine and feminine in the 007 saga. What is the impact of the transformation of bodies on the gendered vision in cinema? What consequences does the metamorphosis of beings have on the representation of the relationships between men and women on the screen? How can we also question the norms and imperatives of domination and open a space for the lesbian, gay or transgender movements?

The game of masks and plural identities is part of the erotic and aesthetic imagination of the James Bond saga. What is then the place of the series 007 in the feminist theories, the queer question, the reflection developed in the *gender studies* or the *lesbian, gay, bisexual and transgender studies*? Is it not then in this framework of analysis that, in a certain way, the current and last female James Bond films have been able to reappropriate the figure of the secret agent and to proceed to a certain inversion of the places and the roles?

If the symbols of the virile male and the sultry seductress have a political, social, cultural, economic or artistic dimension, the relationship of these symbols in the work of James Bond revolves around the question of the game of seduction: who seduces whom? To seduce or to be seduced? Which perception takes over, using the body, language, emotion or the look? In the interstice that constitutes the exchange or the confrontation between the feminine and the masculine, the 007 saga offers a multiplicity of perspectives: in particular an innovative plasticity and a capacity of resistance against myths and stereotypes. And, if we look closely, the James Bond films accompany the various women's liberation movements, announcing the militancy, activism, emancipation and deliverance of feminism and lesbianism.

Long before the eruption of the #MeToo movement, launched by the activist Tarama Burke and then by the actress Alyssa Milano in 2017, against harassment, sexual assault, violence against women, the issue of feminism is at the heart of the 1964 film, this four years before the revolutionary movements of May 1968. Far from the "macho" cliché that sticks to the skin of 007 as a dominant heterosexual and sure of himself, against normativity and stereotypes, Bond gets rid of domination, heterosexism and machismo. Yes, in contrast to the sexist image of the secret agent, the film *Goldfinger* places 007 at the heart of *New Gender Politics*. How to allow instability, to operate shifts and to multiply the blurring? How to put in crisis the binary opposition of male and female positions?

The confusion of identities, places and genders is embodied by Pussy Galore, a character who claims emancipation, fluidity and freedom. She leaves the traditional image of 007's muse, languid and fragile, of her passivity. Through her various sexual and sentimental identities, she blurs the boundaries between pansexuality and bisexuality, questions feminine and masculine norms, and sketches out *drag*, transgender and *queer* perspectives in the film. The *queer* movement, which denounces the patriarchal category of "woman", deconstructs the dichotomy between homosexuality and heterosexuality. From this point of view, in 1964, the iconic and heroic figures of *Goldfinger* are not men, nor James Bond nor Felix Leiter, but the women pilots of the feminist team of Pussy Galore.

Modern and free, independent and pragmatic, Pussy Galore is a committed lesbian and feminist activist. At the head of her own air fleet, she is a chief pilot, expert in high-flying acrobatic figures that she teaches to the other members of her team. All dressed in black, the intrepid aerialists of *Pussy Galore's Flying Circus* form an aerial squadron or flotilla.

In addition, this former trapeze artist has a high level of skill in martial arts, including judo and ju-jitsu. She confronts 007 in a famous hand-to-hand combat scene in the hayloft of a barn at the heart of Goldfinger's ranch. During her close combat, hand-to-hand, Pussy Galore handles with elegance and power the physical strength and the technical mastery. She shows a sense of balance and economy of blow - she does not physically hurt James Bond, perhaps only his self-esteem. She excels in the reactivity of defense-attack: using a throwing technique with arms and legs called *nage waza*, Pussy Galore lifts James Bond, knocks him down with a clean, precise blow and throws him to the ground, his precipitous fall fortunately cushioned by straw and hay.

A sensitive being as well as a determined individual, she possesses both heart and fighting spirit, calm and fury. Pussy Galore handles tenderness and violence, possesses vulnerability and solidity, engages in love and war, masters airplane piloting and the martial art of ju-jitsu. Her action and commitment in *Goldfinger* show how democratic struggle, political thought and sexual liberation are linked. Discreet and direct, Pussy Galore is an exceptional heroine: her existence is a resistance.

Embodying feminine self-defense as a new relationship to the world, her singularity combines experience and subjectivity to teach activists to defend themselves. Pussy Galore puts into action, in *Goldfinger,* a new practice of self, mental and corporal, and develops another politics of transformation of the female subject.

During the first meeting of Pussy Galore with 007, in the private jet of Goldfinger, the roles are modified, the places are reversed. Pussy Galore has the upper hand on 007, she dominates him and directs the conversation during this scene.

Pussy Galore is standing, James Bond is sitting; she holds him at gunpoint, he sips a vodka Martini cocktail; she checks the charts and the flight plan, stands near the cockpit at the front of the plane; he spins in his chair, ignores the destination, wonders where the plane is going and is in the background, behind her; the camera captures 007 in a bird's-eye view, above, while it films the unparalleled pilot in a low-angle view, from below, giving the impression that the man holding the glass is smaller than the woman holding the gun

To try to seduce her, 007 asks her if he can remake himself a beauty in front of the mirror and retires in the bathroom of the plane in order to change. Pussy Galore answers him with the smile that she grants him this permission, but that it is well lost for him. "I'm immune," Pussy Galore tells him, oblivious to his grandstanding and manly charm act. When Bond emerges from the bathroom, having put on an appropriate gown, Galore laughs at him and runs the point of her gun across his chin, indicating that he has shaved closely. Bond seems helpless in the face of the squadron leader's confidence and aplomb. Multiplying the shifts and blurs, the duet between Pussy Galore and James Bond puts in crisis the opposition of the classical modes of the masculine and the feminine. Their relationship dismantles the rigid boundaries between man and woman.

If the Pussy Galore troupe prefigures and announces the Women's Liberation Movement (MLF), created in 1970, the close guard of the voltigeuses evokes other movements, in a broader way. While the Suffragettes Self-Defense Club opened its doors in 1909 in the Kensington district of London - to offer courses in art, aesthetic expression, but also self-defense workshops - the secret British close protection team, the Bodyguard Society, also developed. Born in the 1910s in England, this troupe of committed activists is also called

"Amazons". Closer to the date of the film's release, we can also mention the creation of NOW, National Organization for Women, by Kay Clarenbach and Betty Friedan, on June 29, 1966, for civil rights and against discrimination. Or, closer to us, we can think of ecofeminism, *queer* feminism or feminism for the 99%, defended by the critical theorist Nancy Frazer. In the era of the multiplication of distribution networks and platforms, activism is changing and transforming.

But the Pussy Galore group may also echo the Pussy Riot: in 2012, the Russian feminist and environmental punk rock group, the Pussy Riot, performs an artistic performance in the Moscow Cathedral of Christ the Savior, revisiting, in the form of a happening, a *Te Deum*. Following this aesthetic experience, three members of the group are sentenced to two years in a camp in Siberia. This sentence causes a worldwide scandal. Later, after their release, the feminist artists launch the movement "Justice Zone", a digital platform to support and help women prisoners in Russia.

Thus, against a conventional and normative society, the fighters of Pussy Galore, the queen of the Amazons, come to upset the codes and abolish the rules.

In the kingdom of Octopussy

How do James Bond films put forward complex and singular female characters, in order to experiment with a new style of the feminine? If the individual subject is always projected in front of oneself, in a game of mirrors that is never closed, the female identities in the 007 saga are not closed, but open to multiplicity. They engage a process of construction and renewal that shakes up stereotypes and clichés. Through emblematic figures, in the image of uncommon heroines such as the character of May Day in *Dangerously Yours*, do we then witness the infinite dynamization of sexual difference?

In the wake of Judith Butler's reflection on the "disorder in gender" - the philosopher reminds us of the extent to which sexual roles are provisional, momentary, constructed and allow the emergence of new collective, individual and minority subjects - the fictional saga of James Bond questions the articulation of identities and determinations. "I am stateless," Octopussy tells James Bond, signaling that she belongs to no territory and that she wishes to live outside of norms and borders.

If Pussy Galore prefigures in 1964 the creation of committed movements such as the Women's Lib in 1970 or signals the new works of reflection of Monique Wittig in *Le Corps lesbien* in 1973, the militant feminism of Octopussy evokes another group committed to the fight of women, the appearance of " Femen " in 2008. Created by committed personalities such as Anna Hutsol and Inna Shevchenko, the Femen feminist movement was born in post-communist Ukraine. These activists fight against the authoritarian patriarchy and against commercial liberalism. For them, the body is not a sexual object, but a political weapon. The action of Femen participates in the renewal of female activism. Fearless and free Amazons, the international activists of the Femen group are perhaps the latest James Bond, even if, once again, radical *sexism* also has its limits. How to articulate political action and aesthetic performance, how to balance raising awareness and denouncing abuses, in order to alert the population to violence against women? The role of Femen is essential.

For her part, in fiction, Octopussy is a charismatic figure who embodies the free and independent woman. "Octopussy" is the nickname of Octavia Charlotte Smythe. She is both the director of an international circus and the leader of a female gang of smugglers and traffickers of stolen jewelry. A spiritual and military leader, she lives surrounded by women and inhabits the floating palace off the lake in Udaipur, India. A leader and guru, protective guide and influential woman, she brings discipline of mind and body to the community of women around her. She offers a true way of life to her all-female team. To protect the lives and integrity of the women around her, Octopussy trains her followers in self-defense and independence. As the leader of the female commando, Octopussy leads the fight. Her troop attacks the Monsoon Palace of Kamal Khan in India. He has attempted to hijack and use *Octopussy's Circus* to carry out an attack on the U.S. military airbase in Feldstadt.

In Octopussy, independent women are as much accomplished artists as they are formidable fighters. They are acrobatic allies and expert hand-to-hand combatants, like another woman of action, Magda, the smuggler and Octopussy's right-hand woman.

It is also in India, in Calcutta, that the postcolonial theorist Gayatri Chakravorty Spivak was born, committed to the defense of "subaltern" women. In the struggle for recognition, the subaltern woman is excluded from discourse and representation, stripped of her cultural and social identity. Spivak contributes to give back to the woman a face, an autonomous expression and a capacity of action. Deprived of imagination and subjectivity, the subaltern woman is forced to speak the patriarchal language and to define herself as the other of the Western and male subject. Spivak denounces the imperialist violence that prevents the independence of the female word.

By modifying the vision of cultural identities, postcolonial thought upsets simplistic oppositions based on modes of subjectivation and, beyond that, proposes a new reflection in a globalized world. In the wake of Gayatri Spivak's thinking, is Octopussy not a postcolonial activist? By offering women a place of residence and training, the floating palace, Octopussy attempts to bring women out of their subaltern state. In her own way, Octopussy explains that if a woman struggling against subalternity engages in an act of resistance without an infrastructure to acknowledge it, she is acting in vain. On the one hand, literary theorist Gayatri Spivak presents "efforts to give subalterns a voice in history" in *Can Subalterns Talk?* On the other hand, the heroine Octopussy explains to Bond about the marginalized girls she has collected from Southeast

Asia: "I train them. I'm making them liberated women, free women at the same time.

Thus, in the middle of the fights, the affronts and the virile actions of the masculine espionage, the saga of 007 multiplies the tensions and transformations that reflect the spaces of recreation of the feminine to the infinite.

Volcanic and subversive, James Bond cinema can, in its own way, be transgressive: the films displace the masculine and feminine imaginary, or modify the territories of the corporeal and the sexual.

Long before the new agent 00 is embodied by an African-American woman in *Dying Can Wait* in 2020, a new spy and recruit of MI6 with the "license to kill", James Bond is already several women, in the image of multiple and intrepid adventurers like Pussy Galore or Octopussy. The world of espionage itself is changing, as shown by the increasing role of women in the reality of international espionage. Thus, today, the new figure of the secret services, the young Russian Anna Chapman-Kushchenko. Mata Hari with green eyes. She worked in the United Kingdom for the Foreign Intelligence Service of the Russian Federation (SVR). A star of espionage, she also renewed the techniques of surveillance and clandestine operations.

In the era of #MeToo, fifty-eight years separate the two female characters of *James Bond vs. Doctor No* and *Die Can Wait*. On one side Honey Rider, played by Ursula Andress, on the other Nomi, played by Lashana Lynch. From one film to another, the feminization of the James Bond saga continues.

In the context of the struggle for the recognition and the claim of identity or minority positions within the political and social field, the classic masculine figure of Bondian virility is gradually being replaced by a feminine and feminist plural. The 007 saga is in the air of time.

Thus, and this is undoubtedly the ultimate secret of James Bond's adventures, the secret of secrets, like a sixth and final mystery finally revealed: playing with repetition as well as the unexpected, 007's films establish codes that they immediately overturn. Emergence, resurgence, sequence of figures and rupture of styles. Even as it creates a well-defined genre, like a structure established to last and repeat itself, the cinema of the British spy transgresses the aesthetic norms that it has just created. Avant-garde, political and feminist cinema, the cinematographic work inspired by Ian Fleming's character offers viewers around the world a surprising and salutary visual plasticity. Why disrupt the routine, provoke the deviation, break the repetition? To emancipate us and take us elsewhere.

By reinventing the relations between the action, the suspense and the characters, the aesthetics of 007 draws a new type of cinema. Without freezing the show in conventional artifices, the James Bond saga innovates constantly. The film offers a dynamic and proposes a movement, but follows a well mastered score, which carries us towards a world of differences, freedoms and emancipation.

Variations of an invariant, well done James!

AFTERWORD.
THE NIGHT EYE

When I was in hypokhâgne at the lycée Louis-le-Grand in Paris, I went every Thursday evening to the school's film club. It was a privileged weekly pleasure between the philosophy class on Thursday afternoon, an annual reading of Kant's *Critique of Pure Reason*, and the weekend revision programs, devoted to literature, history or Latin.

Despite the intensity of this training, I never deviated from the ritual I had set for myself: discovering a new film every week in the high school auditorium, which was transformed for the occasion into a screening room. We were often only four or five spectators, sometimes much more. But what intense memories! Film after film, session after session, the pleasure of discovery grew.

And the cinematographic adventure, underground and a little clandestine, lived as a parallel path, traced its way, in counterpoint of the ordered learning of the hypokhâgne.

Twenty years later, I still have the notebook, still preserved, dedicated to these films and that I used to fill in in my study room, as soon as the viewing was over. It contains my personal remarks and comments, fed by discussions between students at the end of the cine-club, completed by a simplified technical sheet, based on the reading of *History of World Cinema*.

A reference work, Georges Sadoul's book allowed me to happily find indispensable information on the conditions of directing, shooting and production. Pioneer of a subjective and critical history of cinema, Sadoul mixed economic analyses with his political considerations on the works. Prefaced by Henri Langlois, founder of the Cinémathèque française, this book, so precious for the great classics of cinema, stopped at the 1970s in the reprint I owned. For the more recent films, I had to find something else.

Even today, relying here and there on my notes, I remember the order of the films programmed that year at the Louis-le-Grand film club: *The Splendor of the Ambersons* by Orson Welles, screened in September, just after the beginning of the school year, then *The Drum* by Schlöndorff, *Drôle de drame* by Marcel Carné, *Haute Pègre* by Lubitsch, *The Bathroom* by John Lvoff, Eisenstein's *Alexander Nevsky*, Kieslowski's *Amator*, Chaplin's *Monsieur Verdoux*, *Battleship Potemkin*, another Eisenstein, Ken Loach's *Family Life*, Bergman's *The Seventh Seal*, Nanni Moretti's *Diary*, and a few others.

Among this list, the seventh one screened was a 1931 spy film, *Agent X-27*. Josef von Sternberg portrays a prostitute in the guise of Marlene Dietrich. Hired in Vienna in 1915 by the Austrian secret service, her mission is to discover a traitor in the pay of the Russians during the Great War.

During a breathtaking carnival scene, the vamp makes contact with the Russian spy. She seduces him and discovers his stratagem, which consists of receiving his instructions and then transmitting secret information in return, concealing them in cigarette paper.

Once the traitor is confounded, the second part of the film takes place between Russia and Austria. This time, our heroine falls in love with a Russian colonel, to the point of sacrificing herself for him. She thus helps the enemy officer to escape from prison and is condemned for treason. The repetition of the events, unmasking or being unmasked, mirroring each other in the two parts of the film, serves a refined expressionism.

von Sternberg's film is one of the great classics of the spy film, such as Fritz Lang's *Spione*, which opens with a dilapidated sidewalk and a stroll through Berlin. It also foreshadows in its own way Alfred Hitchcock's *The Secret Agent*, an "adventure film with a negative purpose" as defined by the director in his dialogue with François Truffaut, in which the hero is reluctant to shoot the enemy spy during his mission. These three films belong to the same period of cinema, made in 1928 (Lang), in 1931 (von Sternberg) and in 1936 (Hitchcock).

Agent X-27 prefigures, by its baroque and wild formalism, by the sensual aesthetics and the disturbing charm which emanate from its main character, the spy played by Marlene Dietrich, another cinematographic universe, that of the secret agent and popular hero James Bond.

This comes from the fact that in parallel to the film club and the tribulations of agent X-27, inspired by the life of Mata Hari - *mata hari* designating in Malay the "eye of the day", the sun -, I shared another cinematographic pleasure within the framework, this time, of the family circle: to watch with my sister, my brothers and my parents, in the same shared enthusiasm, the adventures of 007 on VCR.

Two pleasures of the seventh art: on the one hand, the visual for the daytime eye, *mata hari* at Louis-le-Grand, and, on the other, the screen on the nighttime eye, James Bond in the family circle. Two games of the image, *goldeneye* or *darknesseye*? But should we continue to oppose auteur cinema to popular cinema? Why maintain this distinction, within the multiple creations, between the artistic quality of demanding cinema and the quantity of *mainstream* blockbusters? My personal experience, which combines film club and family cinema, invites us to bring the different projects closer together and to conclude that we must go beyond the opposition between the signed work *versus* the open work.

The reflection that I propose on cinema consists in elaborating bridges to go from one film to another, to establish bridges between the work that rests on the requirement, the audacity of a devouring, intractable director, and the creation that maintains the ingenuity of the look.

For many viewers around the world, the international action film seems anonymous. It would maintain the idea of an absence of artistic signature and of the imprint of the mise en scène, by putting at the service of this anonymity and ingenuity technical and spectacular, narrative and inventive, financial and commercial means, capable of seducing different audiences in the four corners of the planet.

Yet, if one accepts to pay astonishing and astonished attention to the smallest detail of the cinematographic image, and if one takes the trouble to scrutinize precisely the philosophical element in the visual scene itself, then, suddenly, the reasons that grace, pleasure and magic are always there appear. The successful meeting of art and commerce, the prodigious pact of the excessive and the extraordinary, the subtle play of the childish and the marvelous, the sweet alliance of action and emotion, the mix of violence and beauty, the association between fragility and strength, and the duo of glamour and suspense. These are also the secrets of the Bondian landscape, symphonic poem and Greek tragedy mixed. A landscape made to last a long time. *Once upon a time in 007 story.*

TABLE OF CONTENTS

Best sellers Max Milo Editions

Hitler's banker, Jean-François Bouchard

Confessions of a forger, Éric Piedoie Le Tiec

The Koran and the flesh, Ludovic-Mohamed Zahed

Governing by fake news, Jacques Baud

Governing by chaos, Collectif

A political history of food, Paul Ariès

Mad in U.S.A.: The ravages of the "American model", Michel Desmurget

Mondial soccer club geopolitics, Kévin Veyssière

Putin: Game master?, Jacques Braud

Treatise on the three impostors: Moses, Jesus, Muhammad, The Spirit of Spinoza

TV Lobotomy, Michel Desmurget